Rev. Seth Noble

A REVOLUTIONARY WAR SOLDIER'S
PROMISE OF AMERICA
and
The Founding of Bangor, Maine
and Columbus, Ohio

Carol B. Smith Fisher
Bangor and Camden, Maine

Foreword by
Ambassador John Joseph Noble
Ottawa, Ontario, Canada

INCLUDING MAPS, EARLY DOCUMENTS, SERMONS, SHEET MUSIC,
DEPOSITION OF THE 1777 BATTLE OF MACHIAS, MAINE,
AND NEW INFORMATION REGARDING THE 1798
SHIPWRECK OF THE SCHOONER *SUSANNAH*

HERITAGE BOOKS
2010

HERITAGE BOOKS
AN IMPRINT OF HERITAGE BOOKS, INC.

Books, CDs, and more—Worldwide

For our listing of thousands of titles see our website at
www.HeritageBooks.com

Published 2010 by
HERITAGE BOOKS, INC.
Publishing Division
100 Railroad Ave. #104
Westminster, Maryland 21157

Copyright © 2010 Carol B. Smith Fisher

Library of Congress Control Number: 2009935078

Cover illustration from the 1980 mural by
Nancy Jewell, Bangor City Hall
Photo by author

All rights reserved. No part of this book may be reproduced or transmitted in any form or by any means, electronic or mechanical, including photocopying, recording or by any information storage and retrieval system without written permission from the author, except for the inclusion of brief quotations in a review.

International Standard Book Numbers
Paperbound: 978-0-7884-5049-5
Clothbound: 978-0-7884-8313-4

This book is dedicated to the one I love,

Kenneth Paul Fisher

and

to that first generation of Americans

who achieved their country's

INDEPENDENCE

Table of Contents

Foreword by Ambassador John Joseph Noble vii

Preface xiii

Prologue..xvii

Chapter One – 1743-1777 – A Massachusetts Farmer's Son Becomes a Man of God and Answers the Call in Sunbury County, Nova Scotia 1

Chapter Two – 1777-1786 – Private Seth Noble, a Soldier of That Glorious Cause, Machias, District of Maine 15

Chapter Three – 1786-1790 – A New Beginning on the Penobscot River in the District of Maine.........31

Chapter Four – 1790-1794 – BANGOR: A Hymn to Honor God and the Sacrifice Paid.........................43

Chapter Five – 1794-1798 – Mean-spirited Aspersions Circulated Throughout Bangor's Poorly Documented Early History.......................59

Chapter Six – 1798-1805 – "O Death!" The Shipwreck of the Schooner SUSANNAH....................69

Chapter Seven – 1805-1807 – Ohio: A Pilgrimage for the Promise of America 83

Table of Contents

Appendix 1   BANGOR TUNE
by William Tans'ur 1734............................97

Appendix 2   Shipwreck of the Schooner SUSANNAH
Bangor-Boston, Oct.18, 1798. Information
Regarding Passengers Lost at Sea................105

Appendix 3   Photos, Documents Including 1787 Sunbury
Petition, 1789 Kenduskeag Plantation
Petition, 1790 Bangor Petition, 1791 Bangor
Incorporation Charter, Maps, Early Sheet
Music, Early Maine and Ohio Land Records...115

Brief Noble Family Genealogy......................................177

Acknowledgments..185

References – Including Bibliography and
Footnotes..191

Index 199

Foreword

by John Joseph Noble

Retired Canadian Ambassador to Greece and Switzerland

Great-Great-Great Grandson of the Reverend Seth Noble

I am honored that Carol Smith Fisher has asked me to write an introduction to her biography of the Reverend Seth Noble, who was my great-great-great grandfather and the first settled Protestant minister on the Saint John River Valley in what is now the Canadian province of New Brunswick (then part of the British colony of Nova Scotia). Seth was also the man who tried to bring the American Revolution to the Saint John River; who was forced to flee to what is now Maine with a price on his head; the man of God who took up arms against the British in the Revolutionary War; the man who named Bangor, Maine and the man who was the first Presbyterian minister in what is today Columbus, Ohio. Carol's book rightly focuses on Seth as an American patriot and his maligned portrayal in some of Bangor's oral history as being partial to "the demon rum."

    I grew up with stories of Seth Noble being retold by my grandfather, Harry Gordon Noble, an absolute teetotaler, who lived to the ripe age of ninety-four in Woodstock, New Brunswick. My father, Rev. Dr. Ronald Harding Noble, an equally ardent teetotaler, my grandfather, great grandfather and my great-great grandfather, Benjamin (Seth's son), all lived in Carleton County, New Brunswick on the banks of the Saint John River. My grandfather's stories all included reference to how Seth had named Bangor. Another story; related to the Congregational church at Maugerville where Seth had ministered, was that the church was moved seven miles down the river on the ice in the winter of 1788, pulled by one hundred yoke of oxen, without any damage to its interior. It still stands in Sheffield, New Brunswick; its successor church, built in the New England style, became part of the United Church of Canada in 1925 when most of the Congregationalist, Methodist and Presbyterian churches in Canada united.

Foreword

My grandfather had a copy of Lucius M. Boltwood's 1878 *History and Genealogy of the Family of Thomas Noble of Westfield, Massachusetts*, the first Noble to arrive in Massachusetts in 1652. Twelve pages are devoted to Seth; I treasured reading those pages and was eventually able to obtain a copy of the book later in life.

Seth's efforts to bring the American Revolution to the Saint John River Valley and the other parts of Nova Scotia (sometimes referred to as the fourteenth British colony in North America), have been well documented by Carol and in many books regarding the history of early New Brunswick. He is regarded as a "rebel" in Canada and a patriot in the United States. While Seth was one of the three men who fled from Maugerville with a price on their heads, the vast majority of the settlers there (all originally from Massachusetts) had signed their names to a petition in support of the break with the Mother Country. The British had wisely offered an amnesty to most of the residents of Maugerville, provided they recanted (most of them did). My grandfather reveled in the story of Seth's escape from the ever-vigilant British soldiers who had come for him as he lay hiding under the bed of Mrs. Wasson's daughter, who pretended to be seriously ill. We could almost imagine his escape across the Saint John River and his fleeing back to Maine using the South West branch of the Oromoctou River.

Joseph Barker, the father of Seth's wife, Hannah, was a co-ringleader of the rebel sentiment in Maugerville, but he and most of the Maugerville residents stayed there rather than take up Seth's invitation to come to Maine. Indeed, shortly after the early death of Hannah (Barker) Noble in Bangor in 1790, while Seth was in Boston to secure the incorporation of the town, Seth made the difficult decision to bring his two young sons, Joseph and Benjamin, to be brought up with his deceased wife's brother, Joseph Barker, in Sheffield, just south of Maugerville. That must have been a heart-rending decision on many counts, not only dividing up his family, but also sending them to live under the very British rule against which Seth had fought! Seth could not have known that his only progeny to carry the name Noble would come from those two sons sent back to New Brunswick. His oldest son, Seth Jr., was drowned in a shipwreck off the coast of New

Hampshire in 1798. His two other sons by his second wife did not live to adulthood. The irony of the American patriot sending his sons to be brought up under British rule can only be explained in terms of desperate financial straits in which Seth found himself in Bangor. He also took comfort in knowing that the Barker family had been on his side in supporting the Revolution.

One of the results of the American Revolution was that a considerable number of colonists who did not support the break with Britain (over 40,000) were forced to become political refugees and fled in 1783/84 to different parts of what is now Canada and elsewhere. There were some Nobles in this group too. (My mother's family, Daniel Smith/Ruth Fitch, fled from New Milford, Connecticut via New York City, which stayed in British hands throughout the Revolutionary War. They then moved to Maugerville in 1784 and eventually settled on the other side of the Saint John River across from Maugerville. The third generation then migrated north to Carleton County). The influx of these refugees (Tories in American parlance, United Empire Loyalists in Canadian parlance) on the Saint John River was such that in 1784 it resulted in the creation of a new colony, New Brunswick, which was carved out of part of the existing colony of Nova Scotia. There was considerable tension between the newly arrived Loyalists and those who had been there before them, who were rightly suspected of having rebel sympathies.

When Seth's son Benjamin (from whom I am descended) died in 1860, his obituary said he and his father Seth came from Nova Scotia, while his older brother Joseph's obituary (1869) made clear he was born in Maine and both had been brought to Sheffield at an early age to be brought up with their uncle Joseph. Both obituaries list their father as a Presbyterian minister, which he was when he died. But neither made any reference to Seth's support of the American Revolution, nor his time as pastor of the Maugerville church.

Seth's two Canadian sons, Joseph and Benjamin, had large and prolific families, some of whom migrated back across the border into neighboring Maine and whose descendants still live there today. One of my grandfather's half brothers migrated to Boston, and a half sister went to California. My father did his theological training at Andover Newton Theological Seminary in

Newton, Massachusetts, where I was born. He returned to Canada and then came back for graduate studies in West Acton, Massachusetts where I attended grade school and was considered an "alien." Moving back to New Brunswick, they called me a "Yank" because of my Massachusetts accent! Given the extensive interchanges between the Maritime Provinces of Canada and the "Boston states," I am not alone in qualifying to be both a "Son of the American Revolution" and a "United Empire Loyalist."

Religion has been an important factor in the Noble family from the earliest days. Seth's grandfather was Deacon Thomas Noble, an active member of the Westfield (Massachusetts) Congregational Church. Seth was also a friend of Henry Alline, an important evangelist of the "New Light Movement," which swept the province of Nova Scotia, including Maugerville, in the late 1770's and early 1780's. When Alline died in New Hampton, New Hampshire in 1784, Seth Noble was one of the pallbearers at his funeral.

Seth's two sons, Joseph and Benjamin, left the Barkers in Sheffield in about 1815 and moved up the Saint John River to Carleton County. They became converts to the Free Christian Baptist Church, in which Benjamin was a deacon. One of Benjamin's sons, Joseph Barker Noble was ordained as a Baptist minister and lived to be ninety-three. During the last two years of his life it was claimed that he was the oldest Baptist minister in North America. My middle name comes from Rev. Joseph Barker Noble. Another of Benjamin's sons, Theodore Harding Noble, my great grandfather, was a deacon in the Woodstock Free Christian Baptist Church. My grandfather, Harry Gordon Noble was named a deacon in the Woodstock United Baptist Church in 1922 and served as a life deacon from 1940 until his death in 1966 at age ninety-four. My father, Rev. Dr. Ronald Harding Noble was an ordained Baptist minister for more that sixty years when he died at age eighty-eight; he served parishes in New Brunswick, Nova Scotia, Massachusetts and Ontario. On the 200th anniversary of the Maugerville Church in 1963, my father preached the sermon in the presence of my grandfather in the United Church, which is now in Sheffield. I too have served as a deacon at the Pleasant Park Baptist Church in Ottawa.

Foreword

Seth was granted a large tract of land in Ohio in 1801 under an Act of Congress regarding the Nova Scotia refugees who had supported the American Revolution. He died two years after he arrived in Franklinton (now Columbus) at the age of sixty-four. That land passed out of the family, although part of it was given to Martin Bartholomew, son-in-law and first captain of the steamship "Robert Fulton," just prior to Seth's death.

Seth is buried in the Old Franklinton Cemetery in what is now downtown Columbus. The exact location of the grave is unknown, but a stone marker saying he served in the Massachusetts Militia during the American Revolution was later erected in the cemetery. A new plaque for the cemetery notes the presence of

> *one soldier of the American Revolution, Reverend Seth Noble, first minister of the frontier town.*

I am grateful to Carol Smith Fisher for the extensive research on Seth Noble, which she has pursued with vigor, bringing to light many aspects of his life of which I was not aware. I am honored to be associated with her work on my ancestor. I am sure you will enjoy her rendering of this complex pioneer, pastor, rebel and patriot.

John Joseph Noble
Ottawa, Ontario, Canada

Preface

Hampden County, Massachusetts

Sunbury County, New Brunswick

Bangor, Maine

Columbus, Ohio

The life of Rev. Seth Noble is a journey back in time to when the average American colonial had it in his power to change the world. Anyone who reads about this time period is amazed that America actually fired "the shot heard round the world" and then, against all odds, accomplished the greatest shock to world order mankind has ever known. It was not easy for "We the people . . . to form a more perfect union" for "life, liberty, and the pursuit of happiness." The sacrifices Seth Noble made for the promise of America were not unique to him, but reading his story offers a new glimpse into the founding of our country.

This book gives the reader the chance to become acquainted with an ordinary man who rose to extraordinary heights during the most important period in American history. Most American colonials were fearful of independence from Great Britain during the early part of the American Revolution. Seth Noble however, decided early (1774) that America was ordained by God to be the true Promised Land, and he dared preach treason throughout New England and Nova Scotia. This book is about the sacrifices one man made for the promise of America.

My own personal relationship with Rev. Seth Noble began very early. I was born in Bangor, Maine in 1947, very near to the site of Seth Noble's home. Even though my parents moved to Bethesda, Maryland soon after I was born, I was always intrigued with the concept of one's first home. As a child, my favorite excursion was to drive with my parents across the Potomac River to visit Mount Vernon, the beloved estate of George and Martha Washington. It fascinated me to be at the exact location of the home of a man who changed the world so many years ago.

Preface

After I returned to the place of my birth in 1979, I developed the same curiosity about Bangor that I had earlier felt for Mount Vernon. Many walks along the banks of the Penobscot River over the Indian Trail Park on the Brewer side left me wanting to know more about this sacred area. Very little is written on Bangor's early origins, but my curiosity slowly led me on an amazing journey. It has been six years since I started my quest to find the man who named Bangor, Maine, and the result is a surprise visit back to the "dark ages" of our nation's history. Most early histories of Maine concentrate on influential people of means or wealthy landowners who never resided here. The story of our early settlers has never been told because firsthand documentation is extremely scarce.

Recent books on the lives of our founding fathers have generated great excitement, but who made it possible for our founding fathers to take on "that glorious cause?" It was people like Seth Noble who joined the cause before it was barely taken seriously. In his 1774 sermon, he called for a "great American reformation," and even today, contemporary pastor and best-selling author Rick Warren is calling for a new American revolution and reformation, not knowing that the Rev. Seth Noble called for this 235 years ago.

My research had twists and turns that I never could have imagined at the outset. The necessity to look beyond Maine to Canada and Columbus, Ohio made this much more complicated but, for me, much more exciting. His life embodies our quintessential American spirit that still calls out to us today.

Because his life story has never been published, and he has been the brunt of malicious oral "history," Bangor still embraces fables and tall tales of its early beginnings. This book is not a history of Bangor, but rather an attempt to document the life of the most important man who ever resided there. He not only named Bangor, Maine and was the first minister in Columbus, Ohio, he also is among the first documented individuals to call for independence from Great Britain. Before Patrick Henry and Thomas Jefferson, Rev. Seth Noble dared preach treason: "Better die than Submit!" Written in his own handwriting is a recently discovered sermon, showing that Rev. Seth Noble was a man who was prepared to carry a musket for his beliefs in his mission.

Preface

In the course of researching Seth Noble's life, I have concluded that this book will show that our early history matters, and what we don't know could hurt us. Seth Noble has also led me to discover an unknown early shipwreck whose passenger list consists of famous Revolutionary War heroes and a cross section of important individuals who were the first settlers of Bangor, including his own firstborn son. This discovery could be one of the earliest known passenger lists of any shipwreck in New England. Also uncovered was a tragic story of the loss of an entire wedding party on its way to Boston. This led me to the discovery of a letter written to Paul Revere with such pathos that I was compelled to visit the letter writer's grave, and found yet another secret.

Included in this book are copies of the original sheet music of the hymn tune BANGOR and the 1791 incorporation document signed by John Hancock, granting the name Bangor for the former Kenduskeag Plantation. Also included are early photos, engravings, deeds, maps and various other documents never before published. Being born in Bangor, and planning on spending eternity there, it is with enormous pride that I offer to the reader a brief window into our past so that our journey through time is seen as a continuum of the lives of those who came before us.

There is so much more rich history to this time period that has not yet been published. My wish is to have this book serve as a catalyst for further research and greater appreciation of our early settlers who made it possible for us to enjoy the place we now call home.

Carol B. Smith Fisher
Bangor and Camden, Maine

Prologue

The great events of world history are, at bottom, profoundly unimportant. In the last analysis, the essential thing is the life of the individual. This alone makes history, here alone do the great transformations first take place, and the whole future, the whole history of the world, ultimately spring as a gigantic summation from these hidden sources in individuals. In our most private and most subjective lives we are not only the passive witnesses of our age, and its sufferers, but also its makers. We make our own epoch.

Carl Gustav Jung, 1934

Chapter One

1743 – 1777

A Massachusetts Farmer's Son Becomes a Man of God and Answers the Call in Sunbury County, Nova Scotia

†††

Better die than Submit!
America is now involved in a great reformation.

---- Seth Noble, from a sermon delivered
at Newburyport, Massachusetts,
April 23, 1774

A reward of 100 pounds was offered for his head and a searching party from the British schooner was sent to find him.

---- H. W. Barker,
Toronto, Canada

"Third boxcar, midnight train, destination Bang'er, Maine," went the words of Roger Miller's 1965 hit song, "King of the Road," from our dining room radio in our home in Bethesda, Maryland. I remember asking my parents about my own birthplace, and by the way, I grew up hearing that I was born in "Bang'gor" and not "Bang'er." While researching this book, my search led me to Bangor, Wales, U. K., and to my amazement we pronounce Bangor the same way they do – "Bang'gor!" This trivia has always haunted this city, and just yesterday I heard the TV cable Weather Channel asking local residents how to pronounce the "Queen City's" name.

Rev. Seth Noble

My father, a native of Calais (sadly, pronounced "Calis"), Maine, arrived in Bangor in 1941 after driving up the coast of Maine from New York City with his new bride, Florence Irene Bishop, in search of the perfect place to begin his practice of medicine. Their first apartment as newlyweds was on the corner of State and Newbury Streets, across from Abe and Frieda Miller's store and very close to the site of Rev. Seth Noble's 1786 log cabin. They could not have imagined that sixty-two years later their daughter would obtain a copy of Bangor's long lost 1791 incorporation document from the Massachusetts Archives and present it to the City of Bangor.

At a City Council ceremony on September 22, 2003, my husband Ken, dressed as the Reverend Seth Noble, read the restored document aloud and was accompanied by three of Seth Noble's descendants, one of whom sang the eighteenth century hymn BANGOR. Rev. Seth Noble's great-great-great-great granddaughter, Florence Sihksnel, formally presented this beautifully framed "birth certificate" to Mayor Nichi S. Farnham, and thus my new destiny took shape in the form of a journey to find the Reverend Seth Noble.

My parents left Maine in 1948 when I was nine months old, but I returned thirty years later and bought a home directly across the river from Rev. Mr. Noble's cabin, in a place called Brewer, named for Seth Noble's friend, Colonel John Brewer.

Curiosity drove me to research the history of Bangor's origins after reading a disrespectful account of a silly Rev. Seth Noble accidentally submitting the name of a hymn in place of a duly authorized name for incorporation. Who was this Noble man and did he really give Bangor its name? He was, and still is, a product of such maligned folklore that he must have done something to irritate someone. Here are the facts and words of the Reverend Seth Noble for the reader to decide.

Seth Noble was born in the town of Westfield, in the county of Hampden, in the Massachusetts Bay Colony on Monday, April 15, 1743 [2, p. 202]. He was the tenth child of Deacon Thomas and Sarah (Root) Noble and the fourth generation of the English Noble family in America. He was born a British subject of George II in the Massachusetts Bay Colony and died an American citizen in the state of Ohio under President Thomas Jefferson. He was of a generation that literally changed the world and, even though they deserve the title "greatest generation," very little has been written on the average early American patriot who enabled our founding fathers to take their place in history. Seth Noble grew up in a large timber-framed saltbox home, built by his grandfather, Deacon Thomas Noble, where his family lived by farming the land [2].

Next to nothing has been recorded of his childhood and early youth. He was reported to have been a self-taught individual without the benefit of collegiate education and, in spite of this, he was an excellent scholar of Latin. Two of his grandchildren insist that he was for a time connected either with Dartmouth or Yale College [2, p. 202]. Neither institution has retained any record of his attendance. From my own personal readings of his letters and sermons, he appears to have had an excellent command of the English language and his oratory skills probably were a deciding factor in his choice of vocations.

Seth Noble joined the Congregational Church in Westfield on May 5, 1770 and received his ordination in Newburyport. His first settlement in his ministry was on June 15, 1774 in Sunbury County, Nova Scotia (New Brunswick after 1784) [2, p. 202]. The first settlement in Sunbury County on the St. John River (sixty miles from the Bay of Fundy) was Maugerville (pronounced "Major-ville"), to honor Joshua Mauger, the London agent for the province of Nova Scotia, who took the side of the early Nova Scotia settlers during an early land dispute. For an excellent history of Maugerville, see Hayward, *Generations,* (New Brunswick Genealogical Society, Issues 61 and 62, 1994-95) [35].

F. A. McGrand, M.D. in his *A Parson Leads them to War,* states:

> *Maugerville was an isolated community. Its contacts with the outside world were made through the trading post at the mouth of the river. . . . The land of Maugerville was rich, the people poor but proud and thrifty. It was a community almost twenty miles long – an outpost of New England on the frontier of Nova Scotia. The chief bond in the community was the Church Covenant and the Puritan Conscience. The moral law as they interpreted it, was of*

greater importance than the civil law of Nova Scotia . . . Maugerville was midway between Massachusetts and Halifax and its commercial interests were identified with Boston [35, p. 17].

A 1774 Seth Noble sermon found by descendant Joanne Schotthoefer, showed the early seeds of his patriotic fervor. It was obvious that Rev. Seth Noble was not going to remain neutral during the events that were now unfolding all around him [34].

On August 24, 1758, in the *Boston Weekly News-letter,* Nova Scotia Governor Charles Lawrence issued a proclamation encouraging New Englanders (known as Nova Scotia Yankees) to come to the northern colony of Nova Scotia. He wished to settle English-speaking Protestants on land from which the Acadians had been expelled in 1755. Governor Lawrence told the New Englanders that they would feel at home because the governmental system would be similar to that of Massachusetts [13]. Approximately eighty families, mainly New Englanders from Rowley, Massachusetts, left New England and started life anew in the little community of Sunbury, as it was then called.

According to the Fredericton Archives, Canada's Sunbury County was named for George Montague Dunk, Viscount of Sunbury and the first Earl of Halifax. Sunbury is the name of an ancient English village, Sunbury-on-Thames, situated fifteen miles southwest of London in the county of Middlesex, England and is the birthplace of William Penn. The name Sunbury is derived from the tenth century Saxon King Sunna (Sunna's Burh, Sunnanbyrig, Sunneberie to Sunbury-on-Thames) and, contrary to local Bangor folklore, has nothing to do with sunshine [3].

Seth Noble's decision, made in his youth, to go to the Nova Scotia community of Maugerville, in Sunbury County, resulted in an experience that struck a major cord in his heartstrings and resonated throughout his entire life. Seth Noble became their first settled minister on June 15, 1774. According to Hayward:

Maugerville was fairly well established when Rev. Noble arrived. The soil was rich and productive. A church, a school and a judicial system had been established. A trading post had been in place at the mouth of the river for about 12 years and there was trade with Newburyport on a regular basis. Even in 1774, it was not an untamed wilderness [35].

The sermon, delivered by Rev. Seth Noble in 1774 and found in the Andover Harvard Theological Library, places Rev. Seth Noble among the first to have publicly called for independence from Great Britain. At the top of the first page of his sermon, is written the following:

Maugerville, August 11, 1774; Newbury-Port, April 23, 1774; Portland [Nova Scotia], May 7, 1775; Wilbraham [Massachusetts], 1778 [34].

This implies that he recorded the dates and the places where this sermon was delivered. From Gaustan & Schmidt, *The Religious History of America:*

Congregationalism was locally owned and operated and wholly committed to the revolutionary cause . . . [John] Adams wrote to a cousin in the early years of the American Revolution that it is religion and morality alone which can establish the principles upon which freedom can securely stand. Without virtue, people may change governments, but in doing so they only trade one tyranny for another [66, p. 133].

This sermon, written in the form of informal notes, is very difficult to read. The ink has faded in certain spots, but I have deciphered some clear and important words. At the beginning of his sermon, he lays out a premise with four parts:

I. What are common presages of giving people up to destruction?

It is a sign that it is about to give a people up to destruction when Iniquity universally abounds . . . . Therefore we may determine whenever sin reigns unconstrained among a nation or people, we may *determine that He is about to magnify his justice in condemnation or his grace in bringing about a reformation . . . . He deals with nations as tender parents with children with many respects. He begins to correct in mercy: He calls judgement his **strange** work: a work which He hath **no** pleasure, nor satisfaction in . . . . He stretches out his arm toward them all Day-long. And if they refuse to hear his call; He begins to chastise, He begins with some small visitation first, waits to see if they will return to obedience. Then he proceeds **further & further** repeats his judgments oftner & more severe; till at length the whole **heaven** gathers blackness and nothing is to be seen but destruction on every side. If a people will not hear his first judgements; may be he gives them up to hardness of heart and blindness of mind; then destruction inevitably ensues. Sometimes when he begins to contend with a nation, he sends **sickness** or drought, or overblowing rains, or hail or worms; if they take no notice of these, he takes away the first born, girls on his armour almost an infinite variety of expression pertinent to this point . . . . It is a sign that God is about to give people up to destruction; when bribery takes place among the great men of a nation. When men will sell themselves to do iniquity; people are in an unhappy situation . . . . It is a sign a Nation is about to be given up, when a Nation is divided against itself. Our Saviour tells us a kingdom divided against itself cannot stand. If the rulers and the common [people] are divided, it renders the state more dangerous, than when common people are divided only. Rulers have doubtless the strength of a nation in their hands; and are more acquainted with the art of war & politicks . . . . It is a sign . . . when the **Lawmakers** are **Lawbreakers**. In our fallen state it is very difficult to subsist any considerable time; without humane laws. Better to have no legislative power; than to have legislators perpetuate such laws.*

*II. I think it is evident that these signs which have been mentioned is **nearly** the case of our Nation & Land.*

It is evident iniquity almost universally abounds in our nation & Land. . . . And what are the consequences of it? **Contentious,** ___?___ **& Poverty** *which brings on disgrace within our nation . . . to come. . . .* **Lying, Whoring, Cheating, Stealing, Cursing, Swearing, & Blaspheming. Whoring & adultery,** *are becoming almost as common, even among the great men of this Nation . . . . Infidelity amazingly abounds in great Britain and begins to show her . . . head in America . . . . It is evident that bribery rears his head in our Nation, for instance, Bing [Admiral Byng] at Minorca. If most of these terrible accounts are true [bribery and cowardice], who can conduct the important affairs of the British Nation when they are almost wholly given up to pleasure. . . . Our nation is divided against itself. . . . When the* **Lawmakers** *are the* **Lawbreakers.** *. . . In our fallen state it is very difficult to subsist any considerable time; without humane laws. A people who have no Laws, are in a most wretched condition and are so much given up to sin; they stand in more awe of humane laws than they do of disciplinary [laws], which is a most melancholy thing. O unhappy people whose circumstances are such. Better to have no legislative power; than to have legislators perpetuate such laws. . . . Taxation – These taxes do not defray charges and they appease no rebellion! Worse things are coming!* **Better die than Submit!**
I have read a new translation of the New testament. It has become practice to throw entirely out all _____?_____ *. In some parts of New England this hath brought in so many* ____?____ *among Protestants.* **Veto this in Parliament!**

   III. All these judgments are coming upon us.

   IV. What must be done to appease the wrath?

A reformation must take place. . . . When He accomplishes any glorious work, He begins where there is no foundation laid, then work may appear and a nation out of

> nothing. . . . *So when he is to accomplish any great work, he begins at the lowest end when he under-takes to renew. . . . Latter day glory Shall begin in America. If Isaiah (60:9) tells us it shall begin in some remote part of the world and unapproachable only by Navigation . . . this prophecy seems plainly to point to America, no other place as the first fruits of the latter Day glory . . . Prophet Isaiah mentions here refers to something besides conversion with Europe . . . the glorious work did not begin in Europe or Jerusalem. God hath made two grand continents, Eastern and Western, far separated from each other by water. . . . The prophecy seems plainly to point to America and no other place as the first fruits of a latter-Day glory. . . . America, or the Western continent is lately discovered, it is newly created: it hath been until lately in His possession, without a church, a new most glorious state of a church might commence here, (a spiritual sense) to create anew. God, in his providence observes a kind of equal distribution of things, both old and new; He hath honored us with birth and He may purchase a redemption, it is rational to suppose a grand spiritual birth, a glorious application of redemption will begin in America. . . . America has received the true religion and the old continent has been born and crucified. A most glorious state . . . a glorious renovation shall originate here [34].*

This homily is not only an important rare example of an early Congregational sermon, it is an early example of a public call for independence from Great Britain by an obscure, young New England man of God. It is my impression that Rev. Seth Noble believed God had great plans for America. Where did the average future American get the idea that his colony could and should separate from the mother country and form an independent nation? This did not happen overnight. It came as a groundswell. Rev. Seth Noble's courage to voice his treasonist views at such an early date (1774) within the framework of biblical "presages," give the reader a firsthand account of the very foundation of his core beliefs, which guide him through his entire life. Patrick Henry spoke his famous words, "Give me liberty or give me death!" before the Virginia Provincial Convention in 1775. Seth Noble's "Better die than Submit," can be seen as an earlier Yankee version of the latter eloquent Virginian battle cry.

After residing in Maugerville for one year, Seth Noble married Hannah Barker on November 30, 1775, the sixteen-year-old daughter of Joseph and Sarah (Stickney-Palmer) Barker, born on February 19, 1759 in Rowley, Massachusetts. According to a descendant of Joseph and Sarah Barker, Rev. Cannon Charles Karsten of Readfield, Maine, Hannah and Seth Noble shared an apartment in the back of the Maugerville Church when they were first married. From H. W. Barker, *The Maugerville Church and the American Revolution,* the following entry was made in the church minutes:

Met on the adjournment on Wednesday ye 29 of June 1774 And voted as addition to the salary of Mr. Seth Noble (65 pounds) if he would except of our call, to cut and haul twenty-five cords of wood to his house yearly so long as he shall continue to be our Minister. The meeting dissolved [37].

The Barker and Palmer families were among the original "Yankee" settlers and arrived there in 1763. The inhabitants built their first church in 1774 and then turned their attention to hiring their first minister. This church is still in existence today and was later moved to nearby Sheffied.

Stewart and Rawlyk in their, *A People Highly Favoured of God: The Nova Scotia Yankees and the American Revolution,* give an interesting account of the arrival of Rev. Seth Noble in the small outpost community in Sunbury County:

In 1774 or 1775 a figure who was to assume great importance in the local social structure arrived from Massachusetts. Seth Noble, the first permanent minister to be settled in Maugerville, had not missed the colonial controversy with Britain. He had lived in Massachusetts during the series of disputes from the Stamp Act crisis to the Boston massacre and its aftermath and was well aware of what he believed to be the grave danger, which threatened the freedom of the colonies. Noble became one of the leaders of the revolutionary movement in Maugerville. He brought the issues before the people, explained their significance and urged the town to join the American struggle. In May of 1776 the Revolutionary Committee elected to organize Maugerville for participation in the American cause and consisted of twelve members, ten of whom had been prominent figures in the church of Seth Noble [13, p. 58].

The following letter by Seth Noble written to his brother-in-law in 1776 gives the reader a glimpse into this very important yet obscure time period:

Dear Kinsman:

I received yours of the 7th and 10th, with joy. Had you been more particular respecting the national difficulties, it would have been an addition to my joy. I have enjoyed a usual state of health. I took a bosom companion the last of November. She has been pressed down under a weight and burden of her sins, almost ever since we entered into that near relation, but I trust, within a few days past, has happily taken sanctuary in Christ, the only ark of safety.

There is at present a considerable shaking of the dry bones among us, and several have happily put on Christ, which is life eternal. Simeon Towns is daily rejoicing in the rock of his salvation. Asa Kimball and wife are troubled in mind during his absence. It was pressed upon him to return to this place, which he did with Capt. Lovet, and is now almost incessantly praising and adoring the lowly Jesus. Andrew Tibbets and wife, Mr. Gellison's wife, Thomas Saunders, Sarah Coy, and Alice Potter seem under the preparatory work of the Spirit . . . . My wife with myself desires to be remembered to you, to Mr. Granger, to your mother, and all my kindred and acquaintance.

From your friend and humble servant,
Seth Noble
Maugerville, 7th Febr. 1776

P.S. I send this letter by Capt. Row, tho' it is uncertain whether he goes farther than Machias. I shall expect you in the spring, if there is any passing. I should be glad to take Medad Noble till he is 21, except he should be greatly bent on learning a trade, and if he is, I will endeavor to get him a good place at Newbury Port. Pray advise with his mother and my brethren about it, and especially with him. If he and they think it best, pray bring him down with you – I will do as well by him as I would by my own. Mr. Saunders has done considerable labor on your land. We have had something of a cold season of late, though not colder than it is many times at Westfield. We have about eighteen inches of snow. Mr. Makin died soon after you went away, but nobody since. Jeremiah Howland and Polly Buber were published last Sabbath, and Israel Esty and Salome Burpe. Josiah Whitney is married.

It seems to be still as to political affairs. If you could bring a Suffield dishturner, it might be a benefit to the person and to this place. A saddler is much-wanted for there have been near a dozen horses purchased here since you left us. There were sundry opportunities to get a passage from New England here last fall. We have a number of vessels lately come in from over the Bay. We have unanimously signed a paper, to join New England in the national struggle, and are making all possible preparations for war. The fleet and army that went from Boston to Halifax have sailed, we suppose, for England, though they pretended they were going to Quebec.

May 20, 1776
To Mr. Aaron Dewey
  Westfield,
    County of Hampden,
      Massachusetts Bay [Colony] [2, p. 203-204]

After this letter was written, Seth Noble's life would be fully consumed by events unfolding around him and he would now be committed to independence from Great Britain ("this glorious cause") which, he fully realized, would change the world forever. Colonel Jonathan Eddy, who is buried in the town that bears his name, led the siege of Fort Cumberland in Nova Scotia in October of 1776. This first and only military action led by patriotic New Englanders (known as rebels in Canada), who wanted to bring Revolutionary ideals to this New England outpost, failed miserably. The real losers, however, were the families who were left behind to live under British control [10, p.196 and p.18].

In an excerpt from a 1777 letter, John Allan describes the abusive British treatment of wives left behind:

> *I have heard of an oportunity [sic] down River; have only time to acquaint your Honors that a Number of the unhappy people of Cumberland [Nova Scotia] arrived here, being forced from there by the Severe & Rigid mandates of the British Tyrant, whose subjects are persecuting the unhappy sufferers with unrelenting malice and fury. The common appellation is to Women Damn'd Rebel Bitches & whores, Excuse the rough Expression, & often kicked when met in the street. My unhappy Wife has been often accosted in this manner [10, p.196].*

With the perspective of history, one can see that this siege caused the British to view Nova Scotia as a "clear and present danger." The British focus on this outpost area was an advantage to the American cause, in that it took troops and supplies away from the mid-Atlantic colonies, where Washington was readying to spend one of the worst winters in his life. Had the Nova Scotia Yankees been successful, however, this would have put further pressure on General George Washington to send reinforcements, which he clearly was unable to do. From F. A. McGrand, M. D. is another thought:

> *Had the [Fort] Cumberland affair succeeded, as it nearly did, and had the Continental Congress given support to the invasion, Nova Scotia would no doubt have become*

the 14th State. . . . Had the Continental Congress concentrated on the invasion of Nova Scotia, Seth Noble would have had most likely an honoured place in New Brunswick history instead of dying a lonely and forgotten man, his bones resting in an unmarked grave [in] Ohio [35, p. 32].

For an excellent account of the failed siege of Fort Cumberland, I refer the reader to Ernest Clark's book, *Siege of Fort Cumberland – 1776 [18]*.

Listed among the participants in this failed expedition led by Jonathan Eddy are Seth Noble, Jonathan Nevers and Dr. Phineas Nevers [18, p.216]. Dr. Nevers and the Reverend Noble would come to the Kenduskeag Plantation and were close neighbors to each other near what is today Newbury Street. These men had to leave Sunbury County; they escaped to Machias on the coast of Maine to seek the help of sympathetic Machias residents. Seth Noble tried to make it back to his wife Hannah, who spent the entire Revolution in Maugerville without him, in the home of her parents, Joseph and Sarah Barker. (For an example of one of the beautiful letters written by Hannah during this time period, see Chapter Four.)

There is an unusual descriptive oral history of his escape, recorded in Boltwood's *Noble Genealogy* [2]. Another account of this escape comes from a Barker descendant, H. W. Barker of Toronto, Canada, *The Maugerville Church and the American Revolution* (1904). Seth Noble descendant John Joseph Noble of Ottawa, Ontario, Canada, kindly shared this information with me:

June 30th, 1777

About this time a body of English soldiers came up the river in a schooner with the purpose of compelling the settlers to declare themselves [loyal to the King]. . . . but among the irreconcilables we find the names of Rev. Seth Noble, Jacob Barker and Elisha Nevers. The Maugerville parson chose to suddenly depart, but escape was difficult. A reward of 100 pounds was offered for his head and a searching party from the schooner was sent to find him.

He was hiding in the house of Mrs. Wasson, by whom he was concealed in a bed upon which her daughter placed herself in feigned sickness. The lieutenant in charge of the party entered the house, Mrs. Wasson told him he must keep out of the bedroom for her daughter was in bed, but he rudely pushed her to one side and went through the door. The young lady's blushes convinced the soldier that she was in a fever, and without making further search he departed. When the soldiers had returned to the schooner the daughter arose and watched the vessel sail on up the river bound for St. Anns [now Fredericton]. When it had disappeared round the bend, she rowed Noble across the river, and then he made his way on foot by night until he was across the border [37].

Chapter Two

1777 – 1786

Private Seth Noble
A Soldier of that Glorious Cause
Machias, District of Maine

†††

Had it not been for a remarkable interposition of providence, the largest body of our Men; must have fallen into the Enemies hands. . . . A considerable number of Indians were anxious to engage the British troops and shew their attachment to the American cause. . . . When the Enemy attacked Machias, 14th August 1777, said [John] Allan appeared without arms; [Colonel Jonathan] Eddy defied him to take his arms, and hear his Indians. . . .

---- The Deposition of Seth Noble
Suffolk [Boston], July 7th 1779

Our patriot, Rev. Seth Noble, having narrowly escaped death and being forced to leave his pregnant wife in Maugerville, fled to Machias, on the coast of Maine. He had turned soldier, shouldered a musket, and escaped down the St. John River, via Musquash Cove, where he and others made preparations to return to Sunbury County with help from the Machias residents, who were sympathetic to their plight.

During the beginning years of the Revolution, Nova Scotia suffered frequently from plunder and destruction by American privateers. This activity was so outrageous, that it became an embarrassment to Massachusetts. The courts of Massachusetts even allowed Nova Scotia residents to sue for damages incurred due to illegal activity by American privateersmen. James Leamon, in his *Revolution Downeast: The War for American Independence in Maine*, stated:

> To British authorities in Nova Scotia, Machias had now become a serious threat to their security. No longer was it an obscure lumber village at the end of civilization. It had now become the rendezvous for political refugees from Nova Scotia, who issued repeated calls for revolution in their province and twice had tried to invade it [65, p. 92].

Things were soon to get very nasty for the unprotected settlers in the District of Maine. A plan to establish a new British province was being formulated at the highest levels in Great Britain. The former District of Maine was to become the Province of New Ireland, with its capital located in Castine, between New England and New Scotland (Nova Scotia). The Penobscot Bay and points east were to become ground zero for the illegal royal plot to turn Maine into a loyalist haven and a timber harvesting Garden of Eden. I refer the reader to Joseph Williamson, *The Proposed Province of New Ireland*, collections of the Maine Historical Society, 1904 [75].

The residents of Machias hoped that Jonathan Eddy's trip to Boston would bring needed reinforcements and supplies in preparation for a return visit of the British Navy. After Eddy's trip to Boston brought no help, John Allan (formerly of Cumberland, Nova Scotia) acquired the title of "Superintendent of the Eastern Indians and Colonel of Infantry." Colonel Jonathan Eddy has not received the recognition for his military command of the second battle of Machias, and many believe that Colonel John Allan was in charge of the entire planned mission [10 and 21]. John Allan did not receive his Colonel's commission until October 11, 1777. From Col. John Allan's diary:

> When the British fleet under the command of Sir George Collier attacked Machias, August 13th, 14th and 17th, 1777, Colonel Eddy was in command of our forces [10, p. 126 and 12, Vol. IV, p. 48].

Seth Noble can be found in the Massachusetts Militia and is listed as a private in the roll of noncommissioned officers and soldiers in the companies of Captains John Dyer and Jabez West. Frederic Kidder in his 1867 book, *Military Operations in Eastern Maine and Nova Scotia during the Revolution,* reported that Parson Noble preached a sermon on the virtue of this colonial cause in 1777:

> *He was a minister of the place, was an ardent patriot, a man of great energy; he wrote a letter to General Washington, setting forth the great importance of the capture of Western Nova Scotia, including St. John river, and proposing to take any position in which he could be placed; it is probable he had resided there. General Washington was obliged to refuse the request for want of men [10, p. 129].*

A search in the *Papers of George Washington* [16] has not produced this letter.

A deposition given by Seth Noble in Suffolk (Boston) on July 7, 1779 to Joseph Greenleaf, Justice of the Peace, was kindly shared with me by the Bangor Historical Society. This deposition, old and torn, with a missing central part, has been glued to another newer-appearing paper and is deteriorating along the glue lines. With this said, I will try to transcribe this important document. This deposition is in regards to a court-martial to inquire into the conduct of officers and others in the expedition to St. John; Colonel John Allan called for the inquiry himself [10, p. 211], but wrote a letter to the General Court dated August 17, 1777:

> *I have appl'd to Col. Eddy to Call a Court Martial to Inquire into the Conduct of officers and others in the Expedition to St. Johns, but I think he cannot Legally do it [10, p. 211].*
> *P. S. . . . . The Enemy lost with Major Stillman [was] 30 men killed. Their whole Loss amounts, which is spoken of among themselves publickly, 100 killed and wounded. I*

suppose not an action during the war, Except Bunker Hill, there was such a slaughter [10, p. 212].

The information in this deposition came as a surprise to me and no doubt will also to the reader.

Before reading this deposition, it might be helpful to understand the background leading up to the second visit to Machias by the British Navy. On June 2, 1775, the armed British sloop MARGARETTA/MARGARITA sailed upriver to the remote lumbering town of Machias, where approximately eighty families were residing. Machias residents took it upon themselves to seize the British sloop, kill her captain and seize two other vessels. The residents headed by Benjamin Foster and Jeremiah O'Brien converted these vessels into a flotilla for the defense of Machias [22], thereby initiating the first naval conflict of the American Revolution. As repayment for this humiliation of the British navy, Falmouth [today Portland] was burned by Lieutenant Henry Mowat in October.

The British, not yet finished with Machias, made another visit with the Royal Navy in August of 1777. The British had gotten word that an attack was being planned on the St. John River by the Nova Scotia refugees/rebels (Seth Noble included) who were now residing in Machias. British frigates RAINBOW, BLONDE, and MERMAID, and the armed brig HOPE, were sent there to frustrate the plan to "liberate" Maugerville and other Nova Scotia towns from the British. The British vessels arrived below the junction of the East and West Machias rivers on August 13, 1777. They burned a mill and seized a sloop, and the next day proceeded up the west branch of the Machias River.

The British landed two and half miles below the village at West Falls and burned two homes, one barn, and the guardhouse [10, p.127]. They waited towards sunset and towed the HOPE and the captured American sloop to the mouth of the Middle River.

On the evening of August 14th, every man in Machias who was able to bear arms headed to the shores along with approximately forty Passamaquoddy natives. It was reported that the Passamaquoddies first shouted loud war whoops and yells [19, p. 180], and Chief Francis Joseph Neptune, from a long range, shot a British officer who was preparing to fire on a home [15, p.

462]. When Machias residents heard this loud noise, they joined in, and the British ships decided not to continue their mission of the destruction of Machias. Confirming Colonel Eddy's command and a statement regarding the Maine Indians' service, is a letter to the General Court from Machias, August 17, 1777:

> *It happened extremely well for us that Mr. Allan and Mr. Preble had arrived with about 40 Indians who were of great service to us and assisted us greatly. . . [12. Vol. IV, p. 51].*

This is yet another example of the untold story of the Native American contribution to securing Maine for the American cause.

The following is an account of this conflict given by Seth Noble in Boston in July of 1779:

The Deposition of the Reverend Seth Noble

> *Who testifieth and saith, that the conduct of Mr. John Allan, Superintendent to the Eastern Indian Tribes, while on the River St. John Nova Scotia, in June and July in 1777; favoured, either of cowardice, ignorance of his duty, or want of fidelity to the cause we are gloriously contending for.*
>
> *He did not furnish his Men with the necessaries of life, according to agreement, when it was in his power to have done it; this was productive of much uneasiness, among Officers, and Soldiers.*
>
> *_____ about one third part of his able bodied Men with _____ miles from the post to be defended for 28 days; in _____ finally___ [missing due to deterioration of the ink on the glue line] overpowered with numbers; and obliged to Retreat.*
>
> *_____ those flying Men were joined to his party with a considerable number of Indians (who were anxious to engage the British troops and shew their attachment to the American cause) were not permitted to engage, or seek any advantage against them; when, I think the post might have been defended, without much danger or trouble:*

much to the prejudice of the Enemy, & advantage of these States.

Instead of keeping his Men in one body, and collecting the Indians for defense; he divided them into several parties, far distant from each other; where they were to wait for his orders; but never received any, only from the point of British Bayonets.

They waited for orders, till their provisions were almost exhausted; and had it not been for a remarkable interposition of providence, the largest body of our Men; must have fallen into the Enemies hands.

When the Enemy attacked Machias, 14th August 1777, said Allan appeared without arms: Col. Eddy [military commander] defied him to take his arms, and hear his Indians; said Allan replied, that he never had taken arms against the English, nor ever intend it.

and further sayeth not   Seth Noble

Suffolk July 7th 1779 Then personally appeared Seth Noble and made oath to the truth of the above Instrument by him   Subscribed.---

Before me – Joseph Greenleaf, Justice Peace

This is a powerful indictment of Colonel John Allan, who has been treated with great respect in the history books of Eastern Maine. The Dennysville (Maine) Historical Society organized "John Allan Day" in 1998, whereby fifty of John Allan's descendants came together to celebrate their ancestor's life. Is this deposition of the Reverend Seth Noble the result of a misunderstanding? Should this one document be enough to tarnish the patriotic reputation of Colonel John Allan? Oddly enough, I have found that this is not the first insinuation of John Allan's disloyalty.

In Ernest Clarke's *Siege of Fort Cumberland – 1776*, he states that the Nova Scotia patriots were in Machias to plan their return trip to Nova Scotia and seize Fort Cumberland from the British. Allan was not in Machias, but stayed at Robert Wilson's home on Campobello Island. Allan tried to talk Eddy out of the invasion.

Allan "took every step and used every argument to dissuade them but all to no effect." Allan had no intention of following Eddy to join the Attack or even to protect his own family who were supposedly being held by the British. Eddy and Allan were no longer able to abide each other, and Allan was anxious to go to Boston to seek the job of the American Native Agent [18].

Was there another reason for Allan to travel south and head straight for the center of the revolutionary struggle? From John Francis Sprague, *Sprague's Journal of Maine History,*(1914-1915), [21, p.235], Allan left Machias and sailed to New Hampshire in October 1776. From there he traveled by stage and arrived in Boston on November 7th. In his journal he reports that he met with John Adams but, unable to obtain what he wanted, continued to head south – right into the gathering storm at the beginning of the Revolution. He left Boston on November 29th by horseback and headed for Philadelphia, which was on the brink of a British invasion [21 and 10].

He arrived in Hartford, Connecticut December 6th and crossed the Hudson River without being detained by the British, who then occupied New York City. He finally made it to General Gates's camp and dined with Gates and Washington on December 22nd just prior to the nighttime December 25, 1776 crossing of the Delaware River [10 and 21, p. 245]. It is noteworthy to mention that Mrs. Allan and her children were being held by British Colonel Joseph Gorham, the commander of Fort Cumberland [10, p. 85].

The deposition of Seth Noble, the refusal of Allan to join the siege of Fort Cumberland, the detention of his wife and children, and his place at one of the most important dinners in U. S. history, can now be seen in an entirely different light. The Library of Congress has just released microfilm of 12,000 pages of Scottish General James Grant, head of British Intelligence [17]. These letters are of enormous interest to scholars of American history and are able to transport us back through time. This now allows us the opportunity to ask, "What did the British know and when did they know it?"

What is made clear in General Grant's letters is the fact that British intelligence knew when Washington was planning to cross the Delaware and learned it from someone who was in

Washington's inner circle [17, Reel #37] [December 1776, "Spy told Brits Washington Crossing River," by Carl Hartman, The Associated Press, *Bangor Daily News*, July 3, 2003, p. A-1]. Grant is quoted as writing, "It is some comfort to me that I gave them previous notice. . . ." Hartman adds, "Grant's spy is still unidentified."

Obviously one cannot come to any conclusion on this matter without detailed research. This book is not the place for such an inquiry, but the Seth Noble deposition of 1779 certainly warrants further study.

Is it possible that Colonel John Allan, a Scottish born son of a British Officer and the grandson of Sir Eustace Maxwell, became a spy for British intelligence? Another odd twist in this matter is a reference in Kilby's 1888 history, *Eastport and Passamaquoddy*:

> *At the close of the war, [John Allan] moved to Dudley Island, and entered into mercantile business. His account-book kept at the time has been preserved and among his customers appears the name of Benedick [sic] Arnold. After the close of the Revolutionary War, Arnold went to England, and then moved to St. John, New Brunswick, and established himself in business there. He spent considerable time at Campobello, superintending the lading of his vessels with timber. At this time, he made frequent purchases of Colonel Allan, which were entered into this account-book. Knowing the antecedent history of Arnold, and the way he was hated and despised by our fathers as a traitor, there is something uncanny in the picture of his flitting about the borders of the nation whose birth he attempted to strangle in unprincipled ways* [39, p. 438].

It raises suspicion, that a retired patriot of the Revolutionary War would do business with the most infamous traitor in American history. With the availability of the British General James Grant papers, it is clear to me that much is yet to be discovered regarding our Revolutionary War. What is also clear is that in the words of Seth Noble "the interposition of providence" may indeed be the real reason General George Washington was able to bring this war to a successful conclusion.

Seth Noble appears to have been residing in and around the Boston area in 1779. The Massachusetts General Court appointed the Reverend Samuele Deane of Falmouth as missionary to the Penobscots and Passamaquoddies on April 21, 1779. Rev. Mr. Deane was unable to take this appointment. Rev. Seth Noble, then a resident of Boston, initially accepted the position for the period of time from June 10th to October 31st, but the following letter is in response to this appointment:

Woburn, [Massachusetts] June 7, 1779

Hon. Gentlemen: I received an order for a mission to the eastern settlements yesterday, by the hands of Col. Baldwin, but finding its contents so much different from what I had expected, must decline the undertaking. I was informed the mission was to be on the Penobscot river only, but I find I was misinformed. There are such a variety of island and other inhabitants contiguous to the water, those seas are so much frequented by their cruisers, that I think it too dangerous for a proscribed person to accept of. I suppose you are not unacquainted with the amazing scarcity of the necessaries of life in those parts. Add to this the reward offered me, when laid out in provisions or clothing, will not purchase more than one dollar would in 1775. From a friend of those liberties which God and Nature has bestowed on Mankind.

To the whole Court,   Seth Noble [2. p. 205]

The Seth Noble letter of 1779 is a glimpse into some of the hardships of this early Penobscot River and Bay Region. It also confirms the fact that Seth Noble was a "proscribed person" and therefore had a price on his head. It is also possible that Seth Noble was aware of the preparations being made in Boston for what was to become the worst American naval defeat prior to Pearl Harbor, the tragic Penobscot Expedition of 1779. There was a loss of over 40 vessels and many lives. The Massachusetts handling of this failed naval expedition threw this region into total despair. I mark this event as one of the pivotal reasons for Maine's secession movement from Massachusetts, which led to statehood in 1820. This was the wrong time for Seth Noble to take a position anywhere near the Penobscot Bay area.

Many settlers along the Penobscot River and Bay who were sympathetic to the American cause, sought refuge in the Camden area under the command of Captain George Ulmer. All areas north of Camden became occupied British territories from 1779 until the end of the Revolution in 1784 [60 and 65]. Captain George Ulmer, born in Waldoboro, Maine to German parents, was sent to Camden to erect defensive breastworks on a prominence on the coast known by the locals as Fort Pine Hill. This site overlooks Penobscot Bay and Clam Cove in, what is today, Rockport. This fort and nearby barracks were manned by over three hundred militia including a force of Penobscot Native Americans with Lieutenant John Marsh of Orono acting as their interpreter [12]. Isaac Bussell, son of first reported Bangor colonial settler, Jacob Bussell, in his Revolutionary War pension record (National Archives, Washington, D. C.) said that he

marched from Bangor to Camden and served under Philip and George Ulmer [40].

The William Gregory (1731-1824) barn that housed many Revolutionary War soldiers and families, still stands today on the Old County Road in Rockport and is the site of the barracks and canvas tents of Lieutenant Andrew Gilman's regiment of mostly Penobscot Native Americans. This site should be declared a National Historic Landmark for the entire Penobscot Bay region due to the fact that after 1779, Camden became the American headquarters on the Penobscot Bay. North of Camden, along the Penobscot Bay and River, became occupied British territory until the end of the war. The settlers who lived here and refused to take the oath of loyalty to King George III sought refuge at this location. The residents who took an oath of loyalty were then taken to Castine and required to help build Fort George. (See the 1789 Petition in Appendix 3).

1777 – 1786

Modern historians have woefully neglected Maine's enormous contribution to the struggle for American Independence. I refer the reader to John Locke's *History of Camden 1606-1859 [60]; Village Soup Times,* "Camden's First Call to Arms," by Barbara F. Dyer, June 29, 2005; and *The Camden Herald,* "Camden Paid Dearly for Resisting the British," by this author, June 29, 2006.

Recently obtained from the National Archives, from the *Papers of the Continental and Confederation Congresses,* is the "Nova Scotia Refugees Petition," dated February 25, 1784 (M247, Roll 53, Item 42, Volume 2, pp. 412-414) and the letter of support signed by John Hancock and Samuel Adams dated February 26, 1784 (M247, Roll 53, Item 42, Volume 2, p. 416). This petition and approval thereof laid the groundwork for many of the early settlers coming to the Kenduskeag Plantation after the Revolutionary War. This petition, written by Colonel Jonathan Eddy, stated that they had opposed British rule in Nova Scotia and

> *were eventually exiled from their habitations and proscribed by their enemies; their houses were burned and their stock & other personal property waisted[sic] and destroyed; and so implacable were their persecutors, that considerable rewards were offered for the heads of several who were the most active among them.*
>
> *That ever since this misfortune they have been inhabitants of the United States & have served the cause of America either in the field or in such other way as their abilities warranted. That at the opening of peace they now find themselves destitute of a home for their retirement; of property for their support, and of all hope of assistance but from the justice & humanity of your honorable body.*
>
> *To this source, therefore, they humbly apply, and with the degree of confidence in finding relief which they think their singular sufferings will warrant,* **praying** *that they may receive some compensation for their losses aforementioned which arose wholly from a voluntary action in the cause of their country, and this, either by recommendations to the government of Massachusetts ascertain & make the same good at the expense of the*

> United States, or in such other mode as to your Honors wisdom shall seem most adequate to so just a purpose: And in duty bound shall ever pray.
>
> Boston – February 25th, 1784.

The document was signed by 59 petitioners (known as the Nova Scotia refugees) including Rev. Seth Noble, Colonel Jonathan Eddy, and sons Jonathan Eddy Jr., William Eddy, Ibrook Eddy, and Elias Eddy, Colonel John Allan, Colonel Phineas Nevers and his son Jonathan Nevers and Captain Zebulon Rowe and his son Zebulon Rowe, Jr. Also, a letter of support was addressed:

> "Boston Febry 26, 1784," and signed by "John Hancock and Sam Adams, Hon. Delegates in Congress from Massachusetts [71]."

The petition from the Nova Scotia Refugees was granted by the Commonwealth of Massachusetts on June 24, 1785 and the petitioners received land grants in Township No. 10, along the Penobscot River in what is today Eddington, appropriately named for Jonathan Eddy. Seth Noble received three hundred acres of land in Eddington on the lot next to Jonathan Eddy.

Very little historic information has been documented during the time directly following the Revolutionary War. This chaotic period of "nation building" proved as great a challenge as the war itself. Seth Noble's wife, Hannah, and five-year-old Seth Jr. joined him directly in New Hampshire after the war, as their second son, Joseph, was born June 13, 1783 in New Market, New Hampshire. According to the "Minutes of the Ministry and Churches of New Hampshire" (*Congregation Quarterly*, xviii: 283), Rev. Seth Noble,

> *for three years, ministered to a now extinct Presbyterian church in Seabrook. He may have been preaching at the latter place while a resident of New Market [2, p. 205].*

The following is a letter from Rev. Seth Noble to Governor John Hancock concerning John Lee who arrived in Castine (then Majabigwaduce) in 1784. John Lee was the town clerk in 1787 and was appointed customs collector of Penobscot in 1789 by President George Washington. He became town treasurer in 1796 for many years; he was the largest landholder on the Penobscot Bay. He also owned sawmills and had large business interests. This letter was published by the *Bangor Historical Magazine* in 1890 by Joseph W. Porter and was found by Dr. John F. Pratt in the Massachusetts Archives:

New Market, April 20th 1785

Honoured Sir:

These may inform your Excellency that Mr. J. Lee, of Majabigwaduce, is making interest in that place and its vicinity for a commission of the peace. I am sensible if your Excellency knew the man and his conduct, you would never grant him any commission, whatever, especially that of Esqr.

I verily believe, it can be proved that he bore arms against America, both by land and sea, before he went from New York to Majabigwaduce.

I was considerably acquainted with him last summer, and it is my opinion that he is yet a spiteful malicious **TORY.**

The way he procured his pardon was singular and beneath a gentleman. [Gt.?] Rich and Dr. Mann exhibited a complaint against him, consequently he was summoned to answer to the charge; and when he set out for Boston for that purpose, he gave out word that he was bound for Port Rose____?___y [Port Rossway, near Digby?]; therefore said gentlemen had no opportunity to support their charge. He obtained his pardon while his accuser thought him to be in Nova Scotia. Sir, a justice is much wanted there, as there is none within forty miles; I would, therefore, request that a commission of the peace might be sent to Dr. Oliver Mann of Majabigwaduce who, I think is the most suitable person, and would be most agreeable to the people in general. That Lee is cunning, artful, sly, designing fellow, and hath strangely ingratiated himself into the favour of the lower class of people. He is endeavoring to get as many Refugees about him as possible, that in case of a rupture between Britain and America no doubt he will endeavor to have another British post established there. Such persons ought to be drove from these states.

From your most obedient, humble servant,
Seth Noble

To His Excellency John Hancock, Esq., Governor-in-Chief of the State of Massachusetts Bay [12, April-May 1890, Vol. V, p. 220].

Just prior to September 1785, Rev. Mr. Noble preached sermons in the part of Hallowell, which is today the state capital, Augusta, Maine. On September 6, 1785 the town held a meeting and hired Rev. Seth Noble "to continue his services until the ensuing March." In the *Martha Ballard Diary from 1785-1812,* is written the following:

September 6th 1785
Ye Town Mett to Day to hire mr. Noble. Voted to hire him till march [68, p.16].

February 3rd 1786
Clear morn. I have been at home today. Revd mr. Noble Came to Town yester dy [68, p.26].

February 19th 1786
I attended worship. Revd mr Noble performed before noon & mr. Haselett after noone [68, p.27].

March 6, 1786
The annual meeting, Capt Saveg wife & Sally & Polly Hamlin here. Mr Bullin Slept here. Theop-h Hamlin & James Burten Slept here. I have been at home all day. Finisht my [gloves]. mr. heslit & Noble both dismist [68, p. 28].

A bit of insight into Martha Ballard's famous diary is given by Laurel Thatcher Ulrich in her Pulitzer Prize winning book, *A Midwife's Tale* published in 1990:

At the time, Hallowell's new church had no minister. Preaching, in early New England, was both an ecclesiastical and a civil responsibility. A prospective minister had to please the town as a whole, at least the adult male part of it, as well as the tiny minority who made up the membership of the covenanted men or church. Until a minister was called, services were read by laymen or conducted by visiting clergy. Henry Sewall and his friends tested each candidate according to the standards of their own private society. "He is an Arminian; &, I believe an Arian," Sewall wrote after hearing one prospective pastor preach [Rev. Mr. Haslett], adding, "From such doctrine I turned away – and met with a few brethren in the afternoon, at Esq.Pettingills, where the presence of the Lord was experienced in a sensible manner [67, p. 106].

Arianism (Arian) was the doctrine of Arius (AD 256?-336, Greek), The Arian "heresy" denied that Jesus was of the same substance as God and held instead that he was only the highest of created beings. Arminian was the theology of Jacobus Arminius (1560-1609, Dutch) which opposed the absolute predestinarianism of John Calvin. Predestination is conditioned by God's foreknowledge of human free choices. It is not clear whether Henry Sewall also accused Rev. Seth Noble of this label, so it is not clear why he was rejected, but it was Hallowell's loss and Bangor's gain. Rev. Seth Noble preached sixteen Sabbaths, for which the town paid him twenty-six pounds and ten shillings. [2, p. 206].

Chapter Three

1786 – 1790

A New Beginning on the Penobscot River
In the District of Maine

†††

Therefore humbly pray, your honours would consider our difficulties; and incorporate us into a Town: by the name of **Sunbury**. . . .
---- Petition to the General Court
Commonwealth of Massachusetts
September 11th 1787

The following Sunday, Rev. Seth Noble preached a sermon at John Brewer's home and also present was Joseph Orono [famous Penobscot tribal elder] . . . .

---- Rev. Daniel Little
June, 1788

And incorporate us into a Town, by the name of **Bangor***. We have no Justice of the Peace . . . and some people not of the best morals . . . .*
---- Seth Noble
Agent for the Kenduskeag Plantation
May 18th 1790

History has not yet meted out justice to the brave men who with small means and against great odds and discouragements, held the eastern part of the State and preserved Maine intact. Among the most prominent of these men [was] . . . Rev. Seth Noble of Bangor . . . .

Memoir of Colonel Jonathan Lowder (1733-1814)

★★★★★★★★★★★★

Rev. Seth Noble

The descendants of Samuel Waldo originally claimed the territory, which is today the city of Bangor. General Henry Knox was married to Lucy (Flucker) Knox, granddaughter of Samuel Waldo and heir to the Waldo patent. Knox ordered Jonathan Stone, in 1786, to survey and explore this area. His report seems to predict the future importance of a great city and can be understood by all who are familiar with Bangor today. A part of the report is as follows:

> *No. 1 in the second range contains 23,895 acres, and is bounded as follows, viz.: By the Penobscot river on the east and southeast, by No. 1 of the first range on the south, by No. 2 of the second range on the west, and on the commonwealth's land on the north and northeast. This township comprehends the head of navigation on this river at the mouth of the Kendiskeig, is the principal anchorage where is about 2½ fathoms at low water. The great falls at head of the tide afford an excellent shad and alewives fishery, and the mouth of the Kendiskeig is the most convenient landing for rafts of lumber which come down, of any place in the river. Those advantages, joined to its pleasant situation, and the vast country above, to which it must serve as a seaport, must make it a place of considerable trade in a short time, -- but those advantages will be the property of a few individuals, if the first settlers who have taken up the farms along the river are allowed to hold them. There are some tolerable farming lands along the Kendiskeig stream, and towards the northerly part; it has likewise large quantities of open meadows.*
>
> *Dec. 16, 1786   Jona. Stone [12, vol. 1, p. 62]*

It is believed that through the influence of his friend, Colonel Jonathan Eddy, Rev. Seth Noble was engaged to come to the Penobscot River plantation of Kenduskeag. Since the fledgling wilderness community was without an organized church, Rev. Seth Noble was engaged on June 7, 1786 to settle there as their religious teacher and preacher, for the annual salary of seventy pounds. He was ordained a "minister of the people" on September 10, 1786 by Rev. Daniel Little, under the beautiful large old oak trees (which no longer exist) and on a long wooden platform on the corner of Oak and Washington Streets. He preached his first sermon before a large assembly and administered the Lord's supper to Thomas Howard, Andrew Webster, Simon Crosby and their wives, of the Kenduskeag Plantation, and John Brewer and Simeon Fowler of New Worcester (today Brewer) and their wives [12, Vol. III, p. 67]. From the diary of Rev. Daniel Little is the following notation:

Sept. 6, 1786, rode to Mr. Treat's in order to attend Mr. Noble's installment; spent the evening at Mr. Noble's.

Sept. 9, Mr. Noble came to see me and said that Mr. Powers [minister of Deer Isle] could not come but advised the installation to go on.

Sept. 10, Mr. Noble has in the orchard a long platform suspended on barrels and a large number of shading oaks. The church in private gave Mr. Noble a call to the pastoral office, and voted that considering the great trouble and expense of convening a council, that I should induct him into the office, which I did in presence of a large assembly; gave him a pastoral charge and the right hand of fellowship. The people are satisfied without any objections. Returned to Mr. Noble's to lodge [12, Vol. I, No. IX, p. 140].

When the Reverend Seth Noble first arrived in the Kenduskeag Plantation, he was forty-three years old. He came with his wife, Hannah (Barker) Noble, age twenty-seven, and their three children, Seth, Jr., age nine; Joseph, age three; and Sarah, age two (see Noble genealogy in Appendix 3).

They first landed at the New Worcester Plantation, where he and his family were the guests of Colonel John and Martha (Graves) Brewer. Colonel and Mrs. Brewer lived on the river near the Segeunkedunk Stream in a large post and beam home (which is today 609 South Main Street, Brewer). It was reported that Seth

Noble, his wife, and three young children came to the Kenduskeag Plantation with all of their belongings piled into two birchbark canoes, and were escorted by Colonel Brewer to their new log home [12, Vol. II, p. 67].

It is not positively known where Seth Noble's log home was located. Captain Jacob Holyoke stated that

> Rev. Mr. Noble lived in a log house near the river, say about fifteen rods below Buswell's. The first meeting of Rev. Mr. Noble was held in Doct. Neven's [Nevers] house; I was baptized by Elder Noble, when about six years old [1, p.79].

According to Deborah Thompson, *Bangor, Maine 1769-1914 an Architectural History* (1988),

> Near Coombs' Wharf at the foot of Newbury Street was the log house of Dr. Phineas Nevens [Nevers], in which the first prayer meetings led by the Rev. Seth Noble were held in 1786. Noble's own log house was in the vicinity [72, p.33].

In a manuscript written by A. W. Paine, Esq., *Residences of Early Settlers and Prominent Citizens of Bangor,*

> Rev. Seth Noble lived first near Buswell [Jacob Bussell, first known settler of Bangor in 1769] in a log house. Afterwards he moved into a more respectable and comfortable house, a short distance above East Summer Street, between State Street and the river, near the lot now occupied by Wm. P. Wingate [12, Vol. III, p.171].

According to the above description, this home was probably located somewhere between the present Pearl and Spruce Streets and would have had a commanding view to the river and to the future site of the Eastern Maine Medical Center.

On June 25, 1787, Seth and Hannah's fourth child, Benjamin, was born in the Kenduskeag Plantation. Nineteen residents of the Kenduskeag Plantation, and the town clerk, Andrew Webster, signed a petition to the General Court of Massachusetts, requesting the name **Sunbury**, on September 11, 1787. Joseph W. Porter found this petition in 1885 and published it in the Bangor Historical Magazine [12, Vol. I, p.5]. (See Appendix 3.) On the back of this petition was written:

To the care of Dr. [Daniel] Cony, Hallowell, Sir, please to forward the Petion [sic] to the great and general Court, and you will oblige your Friends, the Petitioners [12, Vol.I, p. 5].

It was known from correspondence with Seth Noble's former congregation in Maugerville, that he wanted them to leave their British-controlled area and come with him to a new Sunbury, where life could start anew [13, p.180]. The Sunbury petition of September 11, 1787 was rejected by the Massachusetts Legislature prior to October 6, 1788. The peculiar wording and misspellings suggest that Rev. Seth Noble wrote the Sunbury "petion" himself. The rejection of the Sunbury petition meant great hardship for the settlers. A town's incorporation charter was immensely important, because it brought roads, schools, and other municipal necessities.

In June of 1788, Rev. Daniel Little (the minister who installed Seth Noble two years prior) arrived in Sunbury (as the town was then called) and was made a Massachusetts Government agent to ratify a 1786 treaty with the Penobscot tribal leaders. Rev. Mr. Little sent Robert Treat to Old Town as a Penobscot language translator to request the Penobscots' presence at a meeting at Treat's Falls (Bangor) on Friday, June 20th. The Penobscots were distressed by the murder of a tribal member, by the name of Peol. Peol was murdered on Pushaw Lake in front of his wife and child in the spring of 1787, by nineteen-year-old James Page, during a dispute over furs. A trial was conducted, resulting in the acquittal of Mr. Page. Relations with the Penobscots were understandably very fragile.

Since alcohol had been a factor in the Peol murder, the Penobscot tribal leaders decided that too much rum was available to their young men in "Bangor" and therefore they requested the meeting take place in their village on Indian Island. Rev. Mr. Little, considering whether this might compromise the dignity of the event, gathered together a group of men who were "gentlemen of character" and were acquainted with the Indians. The following men were chosen: Captain John Brewer, Simeon Fowler, Robert Treat, Seth Noble, Colonel [Jonathan] Lowder, William Colburn and John Lee (the same John Lee mentioned in his 1785 letter to John Hancock; I only hope that they were riding in separate canoes!) [51, p. 533].

All of the men were in agreement that the meeting should take place in the location chosen by the tribe. Rev. Mr. Little's committee departed from Robert Treat's truck house (trading post) on the afternoon of June 18th and arrived at Jeremiah Colburn's home (today Orono, Maine) at nighttime. Rev. Daniel Little's journal states that they walked

> *through a trackless wood, about six miles, when Indian Oldtown, about two hundred acres, opened to view, with a thicket of houses on the lower point of said island, just above the Great Falls. Immediately upon arrival, a number of their canoes were manned with sprightly young men, in which they came over to transport us into town. As we landed, their shore was lined with women and children. We walked up to their parade, . . . on each side was a range of houses, built with poles . . . covered very neatly with bark in shingle form, . . . only one sachem in the House of Conference, who made us very welcome, directing us to take possession of one half the room . . . , which was carpeted with fur. Very soon came in all the sachems. . . . Then about forty of their men of years placed themselves in rank next to the sachems, and lastly an old man, about one hundred years [Chief Joseph Orono?], a former sachem was introduced in memory of past services. They then fired a canon abroad [51, p.533].*

When the conference began, Commissioner Little informed them that he was there to confirm the treaty General Benjamin Lincoln made in 1786. They were informed that they could have their blankets, etc., as soon as they would sign the quitclaim of the lands of the river, which he presented to them. The Sachems then gave their reply through Orson Neptune (father of tribal Governor John Neptune) [51, p. 534]:

> . . . Brothers: – *Now we are all here together. When we were at Condeskeag [Bangor] we had not a right understanding of these matters, and the young men were not all collected, and we were pressed to make that treaty contrary to our inclinations.*
> *Brothers: – God put us here. It was not the King of France nor King George. We mean to stay on this island. The Great God put us here, and we have been on this island five hundred years. And we have been of the French King's religion, and mean to be so always. From this land we make our living. This is the general speech of all our young men. We don't know anything about writing. All that we know, we mean to have a right heart and a right tongue.*
> *Brothers: – We don't incline to do anything about the treaty made at Condeskeag, or that writing [51, p. 534].*

This was not going well for Commissioner Little, and so he again asked them to sign their names. Their answer was,

> *We have put our names to many papers at Albany, New York, and elsewhere, but will not put our hands to that paper now nor any other paper forever hereafter [51, p. 534].*

Commissioner Little's reply was a classic example of how Maine's native people's rights were often ignored. He informed them that the Government was going to abide by this treaty and expected them to; and if they did not, they must not expect prosperity from Heaven or favors from the government. Commissioner Little seems not to have appreciated the irony of this situation. The Penobscot natives fought side by side with the colonial militia during the Revolutionary War, and it is they who seemed best to have learned the value of the freedoms for which they risked their lives.

Seth Noble and the other commissioners boarded their canoes and headed for Robert Treat's home in Sunbury (Bangor). It was reported that Rev. Mr. Noble preached a sermon that Sunday morning at Robert Treat's home and, following his sermon, elder tribal leader Joseph Orono arrived from Old Town to plead with the men to do right by the widow and family of the murdered Peol, and he expected the matter to be handled justly by the courts. The following Sunday, Rev. Seth Noble preached a sermon at John Brewer's home (today 609 South Main Street, Brewer), where Joseph Orono was also present [51, p. 534].

From this account alone, one can only assume that Seth Noble was a respected member of his community and was on good terms with the Indian people of Maine. His deposition of 1779 confirms his association with the Passamaquoddy tribe during the second battle of Machias, and his presence at this important meeting suggests a respected status from both cultures. The memoir of Colonel Jonathan Lowder (1733-1814) confirms the prominence of Rev. Seth Noble of Bangor:

> *History has not yet meted out justice to the brave men who with small means and against great odds and discouragements, held the eastern part of the State and preserved Maine intact. Among the most prominent of these men [was] . . . Rev. Seth Noble of Bangor . . . [12, Vol. VI, p. 297].*

Joseph W. Porter, local historian and editor of the *Bangor Historical Magazine* (1887), wrote that Reverend Seth Noble:

> *was of genial manners, and a lively social disposition, the ever welcome guest at the houses of his acquaintances, such men as, Col. Jonathan Buck, of Bucksport, Col. Benj. Shute of Prospect, Col. [Gabriel] Johonnot, and Doctor Oliver Mann, of Castine, General John Crosby, of Hampden, Capt. Samuel Bartlett, Simeon Fowler, Esquire, and George Brooks, of Orrington, Col. John Brewer, Dr. Elisha Skinner, John Holyoke, Capt. John Farrington, of Orrington, now Brewer, Col. Jonathan Eddy, Col. Robert Treat, [Deacon] William Boyd, Andrew Webster, Levi*

Bradley (with whom he seems to have been particularly intimate), Jacob Dennet, Thomas Howard [next door neighbor], William Hasey, [Colonel] Jonathan Lowder and many others [12, Vol. III, p. 68].

All of these individuals were respected men in Seth Noble's Penobscot River community. Most of them were Revolutionary War veterans and members of his congregation. (See the *Bangor Historical Magazine* [12] for biographical information on these early interesting friends of Rev. Seth Noble.)

October 6, 1788 entries in the town records show the town was now called "Penobscot River, West Side." On March 3, 1788 the records referred to the town as Sunbury and stated that "hogs could run wild in town if they were well yoked." They also chose officers for the town and listed Robert Treat, moderator; Andrew Webster, clerk; Jacob Dennet, Isaac Freese, and Simon Crosby, committee; James Budge, collector and treasurer; Jacob Bussell, tithingman; Andrew Webster, John Smart, surveyors of boards; and William Tibbetts, committee on road to Crosby Meadow Brook. They also "voted to build a 40 x 36 feet meeting house at Condeskeg." "James Bridge and Mr. Smart agreed to give one acre of land to the town to set the meeting house on. Voted that the timber for the meetinghouse shall be twelve shillings per 100 or ton, delivered at the spot where the house was to be built [12, Vol. I, p. 4]."

Unfortunately this meetinghouse was never built, and the name Sunbury was also not to be. More than likely, the name Sunbury was rejected by the General Court for its British/Canadian origin. The District of Maine was still negotiating its boundaries with British Canada and the General Court probably did not want to approve a name with this connection so close to our northern border.

An odd coincidence recorded in *The Story of Stockton Springs, Maine,* by Alice V. Ellis [50, pp. 54-55] was that the General Court of Massachusetts was petitioned by the residents of the Frankfort Plantation in 1789 to be incorporated into a town by the name of Knoxbury. To the chagrin of the residents, the town was granted the right to be incorporated, not by their chosen name of Knoxbury, but instead by the name of Frankfort. The residents were not pleased by the court's disregard of the chosen name of Knoxbury so they submitted another petition to name the town Knoxboro instead of Frankfort (thinking the court had something against the ending of "bury"?). No record can be found of the court ever acting on the second petition, and the town remained with the name of Frankfort. From the *History of the Town of Frankfort, Maine – 1774-1976*, is the following:

> *Tradition has it, that at the time Frankfort was incorporating, and for a long time previous, Gov. Hancock and Gen. Knox were not friends, that both were very jealous of each other's fame: therefore, the probabilities are, that Gov. Hancock would not do anything to honor Knox, and had the new town incorporated under the name of Frankfort [53].*

Seth and Hannah's fifth child Hannah, was born on September 11, 1789. The small wilderness area of "Penobscot River, West Side" seemed to be most anxious to try again at obtaining legal recognition. (See the 1790 Petition in Appendix 3.) Seth Noble was, more than likely, responsible for requesting the name Sunbury since he had written to his former congregation to encourage them to start life anew in the United States of America. After the Sunbury rejection, the town must have held him accountable for their failure to obtain the much-needed incorporation. His new 1790 petition hints at this desperate situation:

> *We labour under many disadvantages for want of being incorporated with Town-privileges; therefore humbly pray, your Honours would be pleased to take our difficult circumstances, into your wise consideration; and incorporate us into a Town, by the name of* **Bangor.** *We have no Justice of the Peace . . . and some people not of the best morals, . . . your Honours know what the consequences must be . . . . [Without incorporation] we can have no benefit, of our school, or ministerial Laws.* [See 1790 petition in Appendix 3.]

There is no documented proof why the town chose the name Bangor on its 1790 petition, but one thing appears to be certain – Seth Noble wrote in this name, probably after he arrived in Boston. The original Seth Noble handwritten copy shows clearly this above point. My own interpretation of this document is that it was done in haste, with Andrew Webster's signature written at the bottom of a blank piece of paper for Seth Noble to fill in on his unplanned voyage to the General Court. Also note that the document does not include the signatures of the other petitioners, as would have been customary.

It is not known whether the town asked him to be their agent for incorporation or whether he volunteered to take the trip to Boston to see successful incorporation under the new name of Bangor. It is my impression that Rev. Seth Noble was chosen personally to carry the petition on behalf of the small settlement of 567 inhabitants [15, p. 552]. Andrew Webster's wife, Martha, was soon to deliver her tenth child, possibly explaining why Mr. Webster did not himself carry the petition to Boston. The illusive diary of Rev. Seth Noble was reported to have stated:

1790 – Sailed from Bangor June 21st*

arrived in Boston June 25th*

Attended General Court June 27th* [12, Vol. I, p .6]

*(These above dates were recorded incorrectly and should read **June 1st, June 5th, and June 7th** as seen on the original 1790 petition, written and carried to Boston by Seth Noble – see Appendix 3.)

Notes of Rev. Seth Noble found in the Massachusetts Archives, show that he "visited Boston and dined with Gov. Hancock" on November 25th, 1792 [12, Vol. 3, p.67]. This entry implies that Seth Noble might have known Governor Hancock personally; thus he would be the perfect choice to bring about a desperately needed successful incorporation.

A more likely possibility is that Rev. Mr. Noble felt responsible for the Sunbury rejection and decided that the name of a favorite hymn tune, BANGOR would have the greatest success for incorporation. Who would dare deny a hymn to honor God? This hymn was a favorite during the Revolutionary War and reportedly a favorite hymn of Governor John Hancock.

Chapter Four

1790 – 1794

BANGOR
A Hymn to Honor God
and the Sacrifice Paid

✝✝✝

An act to incorporate the plantation of Kenduskeeg into a town by the name of **Bangor**. . . .

---- Bangor Incorporation Charter
February 25, 1791
Approv'd, ***John Hancock***

May the best of heaven's blessings be your portion in this and in the coming world.

---- Hannah (Barker) Noble,
in a letter written to her husband,
Maugerville, Nova Scotia
December 28th, 1778

My life, my joy, my comfort's dead! . . . But I was blest that she was mine.

---- Seth Noble,
Eulogy sung at wife's memorial service,
Bangor, June 1790

★★★★★★★★★★★★

William Tans'ur, the son of German immigrant parents (Tanzer), who resided in Dunchurch, Warwickshire, England, wrote the hymn tune BANGOR in 1734. William Tans'ur wrote this hymn while he was teaching music in Bangor, Wales. It was included in a well-known Boston publication, *A Collection of the best Psalm Tunes*, printed and engraved by Paul Revere in 1764.

Another very popular publication of this time was *The Royal Melody Complete: New Harmony of Zion*, by William Tans'ur in 1767. Yet another publication was *The American Harmony or Royal Melody Complete,* in two volumes by William Tans'ur (1771), sold by Daniel Bayley in Newbury-Port, Massachusetts. Since Rev. Seth Noble was reported to have been ordained at Newburyport around this time, it is not too great a leap to conclude that this is the sheet music that might have first introduced Seth Noble to the hymn BANGOR (see Appendix 1, on the BANGOR TUNE).

The petition headed "Penobs-River 18. May 1790" was kindly shared with me by the Bangor Historical Society and is a 1952 copy from the Massachusetts Archives. On the back of the petition Seth Noble is clearly listed as the Agent for the Kenduskeag Plantation on June 8, 1790. It was signed by David Cobb, Speaker of the Senate, and sent on to the Committee on Incorporation of Towns on June 9, 1790.

Rev. Seth Noble had given much to this early settlement, including its name, religious sermons, music lessons, food from his well-known vegetable garden, manufacture of wooden shingles, and the care of the infirm [1]. He was reported to have been an excellent speaker and was known to have had a beautiful tenor singing voice. I have not been able to locate a portrait or drawing of Seth Noble; descriptions are all we have, so our imagination will have to paint his portrait for us. He was reported to have been good-looking, medium height, thin, of light complexion, and a man of enormous energy who was never afraid to speak his mind. He was always remembered for wearing his powdered white wig, which had long since gone out of style for all but Seth Noble [1].

After giving much time and effort to the poor wilderness settlement's incorporation, Seth Noble's only reward was tragedy and heartache upon his return home from Boston. Seth Noble's beloved wife Hannah, age thirty-one, died while he was away in Boston on Wednesday, June 16, 1790. She was reported to have been buried the day before he returned home. Nothing is known of Hannah except that she had beautiful blue eyes and wrote long letters to Seth when they were separated for five years during the Revolution [2, p. 211].

John Joseph Noble, descendant of Seth and Hannah Noble through their son, Benjamin, sent the following letter to me. Hannah wrote this letter to Seth when they were apart during the war in 1778, shortly after the birth of their first child Seth, Jr., while she was living with her parents in Maugerville, Nova Scotia. This letter is timeless and speaks to all women. The wartime years alone at home are still an undervalued sacrifice:

December 28th 1778

Dear Husband,

> *These imperfect lines, if ever they reach you, will inform you that through the goodness of God I am in as good a state of health as is common for me. The dear pledge of our conjugal love is also well and claims your affectionate regard. My parents and brothers enjoy the same blessing and desire ever to be remembered to you. The time of our separation (by the cruel hand of tyranny) seems long and tedious. The gliding moments pass slowly away, as they do to him who waiteth for the morning. I received your kind letter of August 31st with as much joy as can be expected in my lonely situation. It gave me much comfort to hear of your welfare, but it was an additional satisfaction to hear that you wanted not for business in your calling. May the Lord of the Harvest make you abundantly successful! I hope and trust we do not forget to remember each other at the Throne of Grace. I hope God in His kind Providence will point out a way for us to live together again, which is my daily prayer to Him; and that we may come out of this affliction as gold tried in the fire.*
> *You wrote to have me come up to you. I should be extremely glad to go, but have not had an opportunity that*

was safe. I shall embrace the first opportunity that is favorable.

It is a time of health among us. As to religion, it is on the decay; but some of them who withdrew acknowledged their fault and returned again.

I want extremely to see you, but when the time will come God only knows. It will not be safe for you to return here except an army comes to reduce the Province. The church and people here want very much to see you. They are very kind to me, and I receive many kindnesses from utter strangers. Neither myself nor child want for anything that my parents can help me to.

O that God would give us faith and patience and never let a murmuring sound drop from our lips! May we never harbour an evil thought in our hearts against God's dealings with us. Perhaps He may appear for us again. I have had many sleepless nights about you, but I hope God will raise you up friends and make your life comfortable while we are absent from each other.

I want to hear how matters go on in New England respecting the war, as we never hear anything favorable from Regulars who are stationed at the mouth of the river. You wrote much more favorably than what we hear from the enemy.

May the best of heaven's blessing ever be your portion in this and in the coming world. I received many favors from friends and strangers, yet it does not make up for the loss of a bosom friend and guide. Your prayers I doubt not I have, but your instructions I have not which are much wanted as the cares and troubles of a family are coming upon me. May we not despise the chastisements of the Lord nor faint when rebuked of Him!

These are from your affectionate wife,
Hannah Noble.

P.S. Major Perley has been carried to Halifax, but they could prove nothing against him so was honorably discharged [37].

After reading this beautiful letter one could almost envision her as Bangor's own Abigail Adams. Mentioned by H. W. Barker in *The Maugerville Church and the American Revolution,* is a reference to many other letters and artifacts which had been passed down in the family, but this letter was the only one which had been published. It is not difficult to imagine the enormous sorrow Seth Noble endured upon his return to "Bangor."

There is no record of her death or burial in early Bangor vital records, so a burial near their home in the vicinity of State Street or Newbury Street is certainly a possibility. The old Fireman's Museum (Hose Five Museum) at 247 State Street reports a "presence" in the old firehouse. Could this be Hannah's spirit? A very sorrowful scene must have occurred at the Noble log cabin on Tuesday night, June 15th, 1790. Seth was still in Boston and Hannah had the horror of knowing that she would be leaving this world shortly. Her five young children (Seth, Jr., age almost thirteen; Joseph, age six; Sarah, age four; Benjamin, age almost three; and little Hannah, age nine months) would soon be alone without their mother or father. Travel was very difficult and dangerous in those days, so even greater anguish would be the fear that her husband might not return. What would become of her children? No record of her death is available, except that she died in their log cabin [1, p.159].

I have surmised that she probably was not ill when Seth left for Boston on June 1st. If she had died of an accident, I believe that oral history would have noted an accidental death. There was no mention of an epidemic at that time, and it was nine months after the birth of their youngest child. There are multitudes of possible postpartum complications, but baby Hannah's age might suggest a urinary tract infection, thrombophlebitis, pulmonary embolism or severe mastitis and a long list of untreatable deadly complications of 18th century childbirth. Why Hannah (Barker) Noble died and where she is buried appear to be lost in the shroud of time, yet this event alone is pivotal in the life of Seth Noble and his five young children.

One interesting note is the fact that Seth Noble sold only half of his Lot #15 from the Park Holland survey of 1798. Is it possible that Seth kept the other half to someday return to Bangor and the site of Hannah's grave?

It was also reported by Rev. George Shepard that Rev. Seth Noble "was evangelical in his doctrine and faithful in his preaching, he unsheathed the sword of the spirit and turned the point upon the bearer [1, p. 51]." Joseph Williamson, Esq. of Belfast noted that the Rev. Noble

> ... *was gifted in prayer, a preacher who used notes, but wrote good sermons; he had both an ear and taste as well as a voice for music, especially sacred tunes; as a neighbor he was kind in sickness, and generous; as a man industrious and a good gardener; moral, too much addicted to anecdote and levity for a minister, though very sedate on solemn occasions – his piety was in the minds of his best friends suspended between hope and doubt [12, Vol. 4, p. 194].*

His congregation consisted of Bangor, Brewer, Holden, Orrington, Hampden, and Orono. As a eulogy to his beloved Hannah, the following Sunday upon his return home, he delivered one of his most heartfelt sermons on the meaning of faith [2, p. 211]:

These all died in faith, not having received the promises, but having seen them afar off, and confessed that they were strangers and pilgrims on the earth.
Hebrews 11:13

It was recorded that fourteen-year-old Rachel P. Knapp (who was married by Rev. Mr. Noble in 1796 to William Eddy, son of Colonel Jonathan Eddy) memorized and saved the following poem that was supposedly written and delivered by Seth Noble to honor his beloved Hannah. A member of the Barker family, Noah Barker, Esq., shared this with the Bangor Centennial Committee of 1869 [1, p. 159]:

The Death of Sophronia, Consort of Rev. Seth Noble
[1790]

Forbear, my friends, forbear, and ask no more,
  For all my cheerful airs are fled;
Why will you make me talk my torments o'er?
  My life, my joy, my comfort's dead!

Deep from my soul, mark, how the sobs arise!
  Hear the long groans that waste my breath;
And read the mighty sorrows in my eyes;
  Lovely Sophronia sleeps in death!

She was my friend, my guide, my earthly all;
  Love grew with every waning moon;
Ah! Heaven through length of years, delayed the call,
  And still methinks the call too soon.

Grace is a secret plant of heavenly birth,
  The seed, descending from above,
Roots in the soil refined, grows high on earth,
  And blooms with life, and joy, and love.

Not the gay splendors of an earthly court,
  Could tempt her to appear, and shine;
Her solemn airs forbade the world's resort,
  But I was blest that she was mine.

But, peace! My sorrows, ne'er with murmuring voice,
  Dare to reprove Heaven's high decree;
She was first ripe for everlasting joys,
  Sophronia waits above for me [1, p. 159].

With the help of Philip Mead, Harvard University Ph.D. candidate, new information has come forward regarding the origin of Seth Noble's poem, "Sophronia." Sophronia is the latinized form from Greek Sophron, which means self-controlled and sensible. Descendant John J. Noble has always suspected that his ancestor did not write this poem, and his ancestral instincts prove to be correct. In the archives of the American Antiquarian Society in Worcestor, Massachusetts (Early American Imprints, Series I: Evans Readex Digital Collections, w 023222), words similar to this poem were found to have been written in 1711 by Dr. Isaac Watts (1674-1748), "An Elegy on Sophronia, who died of Small-Pox." The poem recorded by fourteen-year-old Rachel Knapp is slightly different and suggests that Seth Noble may have adapted this poem to reflect on a more personal sentiment of his own "Sophronia." (Note the original text of the Dr. Watts *Sophronia* is in Appendix 3.)

Also found in this collection was an early hymn tune *SOPHRONIA* marked *P. M.* (Particular or Peculiar Meter, found only in older hymnals and no longer in use). It was implied in the Rachel Knapp entry that Rev. Mr. Noble referred to his beloved Hannah with the endearing nickname of Sophronia. The origin of this name, as explained above, is a Greek tragedy, which was adapted for a novel and a theatrical performance popular both in England and America in the early 18th century. Since Seth had a beautiful singing voice, I could well imagine that he sang this tune to his dearly departed "Sophronia" at her eulogy, which he delivered the Sunday after he returned from Boston.

At the recent burial service of my own dear mother in Bangor, being unable to speak my private thoughts of love and grief at her passing, I too was moved to honor her in song. It is not too hard to imagine that Seth Noble expressed his enormous sorrow and loss in the form of music. Remember the moving 1997 tribute by pop singer Elton John, a friend of Diana, Princess of Wales, who chose to honor her at her funeral by adapting his song "Candle in the Wind" into a heartfelt performance of "Goodbye England's Rose." This was the most memorable moment of Diana's funeral. Likewise, I am sure Seth Noble's "Sophronia" was so moving that fourteen-year-old Rachel Knapp was inspired to record it for posterity.

Things seemed to go from bad to worse for Seth Noble after the death of Hannah. He had the sole care of his five children and the small settlement was unable to pay his promised salary of seventy pounds per year. In August of 1790 he addressed an angry letter to the people of "Penobscot River" just two months after the death of his wife. He addressed the letter "Penobscot River" because the name of Bangor had not yet been approved and he wanted to address his entire congregation including Bangor, Hampden, Orrington, Brewer, and Orono. The following letter was found in the papers of Jonathan Eddy:

Penobscot River, Aug. 21st, 1790

*Gentlemen: Sundry attempts have been made for a settlement between the People and myself; but all to no effect. When I settled here, I consented to accept of 20 pounds less than was really necessary to support my family, because the People said they were poor; still, to release them of the burden, I have been at the expense to collect a great part of what has been collected. Very little thanks have I had for the trouble I have been at. I was desired to draw a Bond for the People to sign for my support, which was rejected and another (unbeknownst to me) which hath deprived me of one half of the sum proposed, I am willing to do in all cases as I would be done by; but necessity constrains me to say, I **MUST** have my pay. I must further tell you I shall look to no other persons for a settlement but the Committee which covenanted with me on June 7, 1786, to give me seventy pounds annual salary; what you then did is as binding as a note of hand. I am sorry to take any coercive measures; but I tell you again I must have my pay immediately. I am Gentlemen, with due respect*

Your most obedient humble servant,
Seth Noble

The above letter was addressed:

To Colonel Jonathan Eddy, Major Robert Treat, Captain John Crosby, Mr. Elisha Nevers; and the rest of the Committee chosen to make proposals to settle the Gospel on Penobscot River, June 7th, 1786 [12, Vol.III, p. 68].

One can only imagine the difficulties Seth Noble faced in the sole support and care of his five young children. The wilderness area of the Kenduskeag Plantation was so poor that he was unable to secure either a salary or land on which to build his church, and there were no schools for his children to attend. His only support, at this time, came from making wooden shingles, farming, music and singing lessons, and whatever his congregation was able to give to him for his Sunday services.

Things must have been so desperate for Rev. Mr. Noble that he returned to Maugerville in the summer of 1791. Mentioned in the papers of the Hon. Stephen Jones of Machias, is an entry that Rev. Seth Noble, being Judge Jones's old friend, stayed with him in July of 1791 on his way to the St. John River [12, Vol. IV, p. 56]. This was the fateful trip Seth made to bring his sons Joseph, age eight, and Benjamin, age four, to Maugerville to be raised by Hannah's brothers. It was also reported that young Benjamin almost died along the way due to the strenuous walk through the forest to reach Maugerville. Seth knew that his boys needed to receive the schooling, which was not yet available in Bangor. His autumn departure from his sons must have been one of the lowest points in his life. They never saw each other again. John Joseph Noble is the direct descendant of young Benjamin, and what a wonderful tribute to Seth's life that it was Ben's progeny who wrote this foreword.

One might wonder how an American patriot could have returned his sons to be raised under British rule. Seth returned to Canada in desperation, seeking the safety of the Barker family, who had taken care of Hannah during his forced exile throughout the Revolution. He respected the Barkers, who had also taken his side during the Revolution, and now he sought their help to try to return to Maugerville as their preacher. He was not allowed to return [35, p. 31].

In October of 1791, Seth returned to Bangor without his boys and was now left with the care of Seth, Jr., age fourteen; Sarah, age six; and little Hannah, age two. These were hard years for early Bangor, and certainly "the wolf was at the door" for Seth Noble. He seemed to have great difficulty collecting money due him. The following letter was also found among Colonel Jonathan Eddy's papers:

1790 – 1794

Bangor, June 7th 1793
Sirs: I have a small account against Jacob Bussell, Jr., which I would like to collect as soon as possible. I find his word is not to be regarded. Try easy means first; and if that will not do, put the law in force.

To one quarter of a year's schooling, in 1792, one thousand of the best shingles. Ditto, in 1793, Six shillings, and one day's labor. If he will labour four days for me next week, or when I shall call for him, I will accept of it; if not, sue him for six shillings.

To Colonel Jonathan Eddy --- Seth Noble [51, p. 532]

In spite of Seth Noble's failure to receive financial reimbursement for his services, he continued to preach to a growing congregation, which now included settlements up and down the Penobscot River and Penobscot Bay. During this time roads were few and he traveled by birchbark canoe. In his journal is the following notation:

April 8, 1794, fixed my canoe [12, Vol. I, p. 140].

Mildred Thayer (1912-2005), author of *The History of Brewer, Maine (1962),* gathered oral history from elderly Brewer residents and combed early First Congregational Church records for many years before completing her book. She wrote that Rev. Seth Noble used to travel by canoe and arrived by horseback wherever he went. Bangor never provided the promised meetinghouse for church services for Rev. Mr. Noble, but according to Mildred Thayer, Orrington (today Brewer) did:

In 1794 the framework of the first meetinghouse was raised on this site. The meetinghouse had two rows of windows on each side, sixteen in all. It had two galleries and a pulpit. The church was clapboarded but not painted. Records state that there was occasional preaching. The land on which the church was built was given by Mr. Oliver Farrington [see p. 54], who also gave the land for the schoolhouse. When the new church was built a mile below on the rise of land called the "Meeting House Hill" the old church was used for a stable for a time and later destroyed by a fire according to some old notes. Mr. Noble served as pastor in this section of Orrington until 1797 when he left by mutual agreement. The amount of money which he received was not sufficient for the support of his family [76, p. 75].

This recently discovered notation in Mildred Thayer's book is most amazing to me personally. My former home of 25 years in Brewer on Penobscot Terrace was merely thirty feet away from this site. I am able to confirm that my neighbor who owned this back lot had informed us of the site of an early barn. Traces of its stone foundation still remain on the site. Wild raspberries now grace the site of Seth Noble's first church on the Penobscot River. In regards to this church later being used as a horse stable, the remains of a horse and three (hand forged) horse shoes were found while digging the basement for a new home in 1988, not far from this site. Mildred Thayer mentioned that Oliver Farrington gave the land for this meetinghouse. Since the church was built in 1794, and Oliver was not born until 1797, John Rider or Seth's friend John Farrington must have given the land.

In the *Dennysville Centennial* book of 1886, a wonderful description of the arrival of my own paternal ancestor, James Blackwood, brings this time period to life with a detailed description of the arrival of the first settlers of Dennysville, Washington County, Maine in 1786 from Hingham, Massachusetts. Since Seth Noble arrived at the Kenduskeag Plantation in the same year, it seems appropriate to include this firsthand account.

The following description is taken from an address given in 1860 by Thomas Lincoln, the grandson of General Benjamin Lincoln to whom George Washington gave the honor of accepting the British surrender at Yorktown on October 19, 1781. General Lincoln was granted a large tract of land from the new impoverished nation, and he sent his son, Theodore, to take possession of his land along with 16 other residents from Hingham. They landed in Dennysville on May 17, 1786. The

1790 – 1794

voyage, commanded by General Lincoln's son Theodore, on the sloop *SALLY*, lasted two weeks from Boston to Machias and then to Dennysville:

> *Just seventy-five years ago [1786] next May, after a fortnight from old Hingham, the first settlers of this town came up the river. It was the 17th day of the month and the woods on the shore were in full leaf and cast as deep a shade as they do ordinarily in the middle of June. They landed the bow of their boat into the soft green moss, which carpeted the forest, then unbroken, from there to Canada....*
>
> *Three quarters of a century only have passed, and we find it hard to believe that it is not all the baseless fabric of a dream; that on that night . . . a little body of men lay down to rest in the bosom of the ancient forest of timber, as shady and dense as the ages could make it, whose silence was unbroken but from the wide swaying of the tree tops and the cry of wild animals....*
>
> *The next day after landing the settlers set to work to put up a log house a few yards from the shore. The timber of which it was made had only to be felled on the spot, and rolled up into the walls and not, as now, to be hauled four or five miles. In that house they all spent the first winter....*
>
> *At that time and for fifteen years afterward, the woods were entirely free of underbrush, and one could ride through them on horseback all over this region   [This explains Seth Noble's traveling by canoe and horseback]. But after 15 years [1801] the hackmatac trees first, then the hemlock, then the spruce were attacked by an insect; and the ground was in a few years strewed with the fallen trunks and the woods became impassable....*
>
> *For several years after coming here my grandfather [Theodore Lincoln] used to ride to Boston in the fall on horseback and return in the spring. There were no bridges over any of the rivers east of the Saco; the Kennebec and Penobscot were crossed by ferries. The other rivers he was obliged to swim his horse over,*

> *crossing himself in a boat or canoe. The woods were generally free from underbrush and a mounted horseman could travel through them as through the oak opening of the west . . . [52, pp. 27-32].*

The above passage is one of the rare glimpses of travel in eastern Maine during this time period. It gives credence to Mildred Thayer's oral history of Seth Noble traveling with his horse and canoe [76]. He might have kept his horse at a ferry location, traveled by canoe to that point, and crossed with his horse by ferry, then being afterward able to ride to people's homes.

The official signing of the Bangor Incorporation Charter took place on February 25, 1791 at the General Court of Massachusetts in Boston. Three famous patriots of the American Revolution signed this Bangor "birth certificate" into law:

> *David Cobb,* Speaker of the House of Representatives
> *Samuel Phillips,* President of the Senate
> *John Hancock,* Governor

(See Appendix 3, a copy of the restored original document, which was presented to the Bangor City Council on Sept. 22, 2003.)

It is unknown how soon the small Kenduskeag Plantation received the long awaited news of their approved incorporation. Customarily, a copy of the original would have been sent to the new town to be pasted on the first page of the town records. At a time when Seth Noble was down and almost out, perhaps this news came when he most needed to hear a positive result of his sacrifice.

Even though Seth Noble has not received the proper recognition for his contribution to the founding of Bangor, the importance of this event was passed down in his family. I have had the honor of meeting six of Seth Noble's descendants who reside in different parts of the United States and Canada. They all had one thing in common – they knew that their ancestor had named Bangor, Maine and they all pronounced the name correctly. Bangor today continues to perpetuate a nonsensical version of the origin of its name. Not even the original date of incorporation has been recorded by this great city. One explanation for the loss of the early town records is the following oral history from the *History of Penobscot County Maine* (1882):

> *It is supposed that at some time when there was danger of their being destroyed – perhaps when the British made their incursion [War of 1812] – some careful person deposited them in a garret for safety, and the rats and mice, having no more respect for them than the British would have had, converted them into linings for their nests. The act of incorporation was nowhere to be found [51, p. 539].*

On behalf of Rev. Seth Noble, may I be so bold as to offer this proper introduction to the city of Bangor:

Welcome to Bangor, Maine

Incorporated 1791

Became A City 1834

Chapter Five

1794 – 1798

Mean-Spirited Aspersions Circulated Throughout Bangor's Poorly Documented Early History

†††

The history of Bangor . . . is teeming with interest and is too worthy of preservation to be allowed to be lost by lack of some effort being made to compile and record it. Other towns of no more historic interest than Bangor, and some with much less, have published volumes of their history.

---- Edgar Crosby Smith,
Early Settlement of Bangor, Maine
1913

Written by Palmer [City Council Chairman], the play, "How Bangor Got its Name . . . ," portrayed Noble as distracted and a little bumbling, though some versions of the story claim the clergyman had been tippling when he submitted the incorporation papers.

Performed before "an audience of third-graders"
Bangor Daily News
Sat. June 13, 2009

According to the Orrington Town Records, on April 11, 1793, Simeon Fowler, Esq., married Rev. Seth Noble and Mrs. Ruhama Emery, both of Bangor [5, p. 296 and 76, p. xcv]. Mrs. Ruhama Emery was possibly the daughter of Joseph Arey and Hannah Bickford from Cape Cod, or Wellfleet, or Truro, Massachusetts.

She was not the daughter of Barzillai Rich, as was written into the Orrington vital records of 1790. Lucius Boltwood noted that her father was a sea captain and died at sea, but I have been unable to verify that information. She was the widow of James Emery, having married December 5, 1790 in Orrington.

The Orrington vital records state that Ruhama Rich married James Emery, and a notation above her name states that she was the daughter of a Barzillai Rich, who resided in Orrington at the time. There was a Barzillai Rich living in Orrington, but he was too young to be her father. David Swett, Orrington historian, suggests that there was an error in the Orrington town records, and they wrote in the name Rich due to the possibility of her living with this family at that time.

Ruhama's first husband, James Emery, died September 15, 1792; he drowned in the Penobscot River and is buried in the Old Cemetery, behind the Town Hall, in Hampden, Maine. In the Orrington vital records, "December 5, 1790 – James Emery married Ruhanna [sic] Rich [12, Vol. I, p. 115]." She was said to have had a child by him that died in infancy [2, p. 211]. From Rev. Seth Noble's diary:

April 10, [1793] went with Mrs. Emery to Capt. Baker's.

April 11, was married to widow Ruhama Emery
[12, Vol. III, p. 68].

It has been reported that Ruhama Emery was Rev. Noble's housekeeper after the death of Hannah [14]. A note from Joseph W. Porter stated, "Rev. Noble married his house keeper on April 11, 1793, a most respectable widow woman, widow of James Emery of Orrington and Hampden [12, Vol. IX, p. 16]." From Boltwood, "She is remembered for being 'lady-like' in her appearance [2, p. 211]."

Two weeks after Seth and Ruhama married, they sold her lot #67 with 100 acres of property in the current town of Hampden, for seven pounds and ten shillings, to Richard Sanborn Blaisdel. The deed shows Seth Noble (clergyman) and Ruhama Noble (spinster) both of Bangor (Hancock County Registry of Deeds, Book 0002, page 336). Seth Noble and Ruhama had a child,

Betsey Noble, born in Bangor on November 23, 1793 [2, p. 212]. This was his sixth child and first child by his second wife.

It is surprising that Rev. Mr. Noble would remarry at this time and take on the responsibilities of yet another child in light of the fact that after the death of Hannah he brought his two sons to be raised by Hannah's brothers in Canada, presumably for reasons of the dire circumstances of his life in Bangor. If the birth date of Betsey Noble is correct, she was born seven months after her parents were married. I discovered a letter written by Seth Noble indicating that he was in Boston during the time of Betsey's conception in the winter of 1793. I have not seen the original letter, so the date mentioned could be in error, but if it is not an error, and if this is not Seth's child, he may have married Ruhama to protect her honor. I have no other way of shedding further light on this event. No matter what the circumstances of their marriage, they were married for twelve years, and she gave birth to four children and raised three of his children by Hannah.

Thomas Noble, named for Seth's father, grandfather and great grandfather, was born in Bangor on July 28, 1795 and died shortly afterwards. Polly Noble was born in Bangor on September 26, 1796 [2].

William Hasey (1761-1844), one of the early settlers of Bangor, gave a written statement of his life just before he died. He was born in Chelsea, Massachusetts and came to the Kenduskeag Plantation as a young man in March of 1781. He was married by Rev. Seth Noble to Prudence Webster, eldest child of town clerk Andrew Webster, in November, 1787. His recollections of Rev. Mr. Noble's preaching some fifty years prior, are as follows:

Rev'd Mr. Noble was settled in Bangor some 6 or 7 years after I came here [1786]. He was a pretty good preacher, a most gifted man in prayer, especially on funeral occasions, he excelled. Indeed, I never heard his equal, so touching, so affecting. A most excellent singer. He could drink a glass of grog and be jovially merry. When out of the pulpit he ought never to go in, and when in never to go out. His religious friends had scruples of his vital piety [His religious friends had uneasy feelings about his innermost devotion to his religion?]. A very handsome

> man, of middle stature, dark brown hair, quite a gentleman. [After he left Bangor,] Dea.[William] Boyd [said] he wrote to him saying he never experienced religion till after he left Bangor. Rev. Mr. Boyd, not handsome, not agreeable. I never thought him a good man – a vile man [12, Vol. VII, p. 148].

William Hasey's memories of Bangor are a most interesting example of parlance and thoughts of the early settlers. The entire two and a half page statement is worth the attention of those interested in early Bangor history. My interpretation of his recollection of Rev. Mr. Noble suggests that Seth Noble was propelled into serious grief and depression after the death of his soul mate, Hannah. Mr. Hasey also implies that Seth had developed two different personalities; one in church, and one out of church as a means of coping with his grief. His belief in his Lord was steadfast and guided his entire life up until Hannah was taken from him. Seth Noble might have believed that Hannah's death was a personal punishment for a past wrong and his core beliefs were now being questioned. Today we might refer to his condition as one of depression and seek grief counseling. The lives of our early settlers contained unimaginable hardships which contemporary readers are only left to ponder. (I refer the reader to the 1789 "Condeskeag" Petition in Appendix 3.)

It is obvious that Seth Noble had a dynamic personality with passionate beliefs and was not afraid to speak his mind. His next-door neighbors on the lot above his, were the family of Thomas and Mary Howard. Bangor resident, Maine historian, and governor of Maine, William D. Williamson interviewed Mary Howard as an elderly lady. Mrs. Howard knew Seth Noble well and had the following comments:

> Mr. Noble was a very airy [speculative, visionary] man, – preached well without notes, – gifted in prayer – a very good neighbor and a good gardener; [he was] a very industrious man, excellent in sickness, and very moral [12, Vol. IX, p. 8].

1794 – 1798

A persistent story of early Bangor folklore is a portrayal of Rev. Mr. Noble's fondness for rum. F. A. McGrand, M.D. in *Backward Glances at Sunbury and Queens* (1971), Chapter Two, "A Parson Leads Them to War," states:

> *If Seth Noble took a drink of rum on any occasion, he was not violating the letter or the spirit of the law in New England. There were six distilleries in Massachusetts, and forty in the little Rhode Island. Rum was a vital item in the fur and slave trade and essential to New England's economy. Besides, it was then supposed to contain great medicinal value [35, p. 31].*

Nevertheless, Bangor's early "folklorists" could not resist the opportunity to interject some humor, and the apocryphal "rum story" was too good to ignore. They enjoyed fabricating tales of a feeble inebriated pastor who was sent to Boston to name this place Sunbury, for its sunny weather, but instead accidentally gave the name of his favorite hymn, BANGOR, which he was humming at the time. No one had ever taken the time to research any of Bangor's early origins through documentation, until Joseph W. Porter presented his findings, including his location of the 1787 Sunbury petition in the Massachusetts Archives [12, Vol. I, p. 11].

Joseph W. Porter published the 1787 Sunbury petition in 1885, and yet the nutty minister story continues to the present. The current mayor of Bangor is today using his "bully pulpit" to further demean Bangor's past and has written a "comedy" in the form of a "historic" play and presented this to elementary pupils as the origin of the naming of Bangor. Bangor should have celebrated its bicentennial in 1991, but instead has chosen the year 2009 to celebrate its 175th anniversary.

It is impossible to change over two hundred years of Bangor's disrespectful image of the man who named the Queen City. Bangor seems to enjoy their drunken Rev. Seth Noble story and has not let the truth get in the way of a beloved "tall tale." Those who seek the truth cannot rely upon the mean-spirited aspersions circulated throughout Bangor's poorly documented early history. Even contemporary writers seem to feel free to repeat and even embellish Bangor's portrayal of their first minister.

In Alan Taylor's 1990 book, *Liberty Men and Great Proprietors,* Chapter Five, "Seekers and Preachers," this well-known contemporary author felt free to further demean Rev. Seth Noble's honor by stating:

> *The Reverend Seth Noble of Bangor exhausted his parishioner's patience when he delayed marrying his housekeeper until her pregnancy was conspicuous [74, p. 133].*

As we have seen in examining the recorded dates, Mrs. Ruhama Emery, was 2 months pregnant when they were married, so any reference to her physical appearance would be absurd. Secondly, as explained above, this was probably not Seth Noble's child. Since dead men are unable to defend themselves, historians and others may feel free to destroy a man's reputation on hearsay, to give interest to their works.

The circumstances surrounding the marriage of Rev. Seth Noble to Ruhama Emery are not definitely known. It is quite possible that Mrs. Emery was sexually assaulted by an influential local individual, who then further demeaned Rev. Mr. Noble's reputation to protect his own. I refer the reader to the *Martha Ballard Diary – 1785-1812* [68], in which she reports that a minister's wife was raped by a local judge who was then able to escape the consequences of his actions.

Another rumor, which I am able to refute, is that a befuddled Rev. Mr. Noble, while waiting outside the General Court in Boston, did not like the name Sunbury so changed it to Bangor at the last minute. Sunbury *was* the name suggested by Seth Noble in the Kenduskeag Plantation's first petition for incorporation of 1787, but was rejected by the General Court in 1788 (see Appendix 3). There has been a multitude of stories printed in books, pamphlets, and newspapers. In recent years, articles have appeared claiming that Bangor was named by Irish immigrants from Bangor, Ireland who came here during the potato famine of the 1840's. Never mind that Bangor was incorporated in 1791, and that not one of the settlers had Irish heritage.

To understand how false rumors could be passed down, we should note that the scarcity of vital records from that time period made it possible for oral history to become the only record. Seth Noble was an outspoken fervent patriot surrounded by many settlers of loyalist sentiments who might not have been eager for him to receive the lasting honor of naming the future city of Bangor.

This brings to mind a question that a reporter from Bangor's local TV station asked me at the ceremony honoring the discovery of Bangor's 1791 incorporation document on September 22, 2003. She asked, "Is there a statue or street named for Rev. Noble?" How strange, indeed, that the answer to that question is, "No." The man who named Bangor, Maine has no street, statue or park named in his honor.

After Seth Noble left Bangor and was unable to defend his good name, a light-hearted version of early-undocumented Bangor history started to take hold in the form of oral history. Bangor is left today with an early history that resembles a "Laurel and Hardy" silent film, rather than a semblance of historic truth. Edgar Crosby Smith, in his 1913 "Early Settlement of Bangor, Maine," stated:

> *The history of Bangor, from the earliest traditions of the aborigines down to the present day, is teeming with interest and is too worthy of preservation to be allowed to be lost by lack of some effort being made to compile and record it. Other towns of no more historic interest than Bangor, and some of much less, have published volumes of their history [21, Vol. 1, p. 31].*

After Bangor's wealth increased almost overnight, making the city the lumber capital of the world, the history of its poor early wilderness beginnings was trampled to make way for the "Queen City."

Of all of the ministries served by Rev. Seth Noble, only in Bangor was there any suggestion that he had a fondness for rum. Even in Canada, where he is labeled a rebel, his life and importance as Maugerville's first minister, who led them to war, has been treated fairly, without any mention of rum.

In the 1869 *Centennial Celebration of the Settlement of Bangor,* Hon. E. L. Hamlin, then President of the Bangor

Historical Society, recorded account books of Major Robert Treat, Bangor's first merchant:

> *In regard to Elder Noble, who was the first minister in this settlement, it was said by one of his contemporaries, that although the parson purchased large quantities of liquors [rum], it was with good intentions. Being a very benevolent and kind hearted man, he was in the habit, when visiting his rheumatic and colicky parishioners, and they were quite numerous, to take with him a bottle of rum, which he was urgent to have administered internally and externally, to those sick people, to alleviate their ailments – and usually closed the visit with a good hot drink all round [1. p. 86].*

The time spent in Bangor was a period of extremes for Seth Noble. He accomplished the successful incorporation for the future site of one of Maine's most important cities and then returned home to learn that his beloved Hannah had "died too soon." He tried repeatedly to establish a church; he petitioned the General Court to grant Bangor the land he was promised on which to build his church. Rev. Seth Noble's descendant, David Clark (descendant of daughter Sarah) informed me of his belief regarding the naming of Bangor:

> *Seth was aware as a clergyman of all the other events going on in both the Congregational and Anglican churches in the new country during the years 1780-90, including the consecration of Samuel Seabury and William White. Knowing that Bangor, Wales is a cathedral city, he also might have had a vision that the Kenduskeag Plantation might become a very important city, one worthy of a see or cathedral city. Seth probably believed that Bangor would one day become a see city.*

Obtained from the Massachusetts Archives are five requests from Seth Noble to secure land on which to build his church. All of these petitions were denied, and no reason was given. His inability to secure land for his church must have weighed heavily in his decision to leave Bangor. In 1796 he preached in Braintree, Hingham and other towns in Massachusetts [12, Vol. II, p. 67]. By 1797 he preached his final sermon to a community where he had resided for eleven years. Bangor owed him far more than an unpaid salary, yet he gave what he thought would be his last sermon on October 22, 1797 from John 14:27:

> *Peace I leave with you, my peace I give unto you; not as the world giveth, give I unto you; let not your heart be troubled, neither let it be afraid [12, Vol. III, p. 69].*

Chapter Six

1798 – 1805

"O Death!"
The Shipwreck of the Schooner SUSANNAH

†††

O Death! My son Seth lost at sea and all who were with him; supposed to be at Boon Island . . .

---- Seth Noble
Sandy Bay, Cape Ann, Massachusetts
October 20th 1798

After my dear daughters . . . I live in hopes that the great orther [author] in dew time will now string the harp and cause me to partake of mercy . . . .

---- Robert Hitchborn
Letter written to cousin Paul Revere on the loss
of his two daughters aboard the SUSANNAH
Prospect, District of Maine – January 4th 1799

On November 4, 1797, Rev. Seth Noble asked for a dismissal from the town committee, and left Bangor on November 10, 1797 for New Market, New Hampshire, where he had been hired to preach for six months commencing May 28, 1798. His wife Ruhama; Sarah, age twelve; Hannah, age eight; Betsy, age four; and Polly, age one; joined him on November 17, 1797 [2, p. 208]. Sons Benjamin and Joseph were being raised by the Barker family in Canada.

Rev. Seth Noble

Seth Noble, Jr., age twenty, continued to reside in Bangor after his family left for New Hampshire. He was reported to have been a promising young man and was universally loved by all who knew him [2]. He was Seth and Hannah's firstborn child and was separated from his father for the first five years of his life during the Revolutionary War. He stayed by his father's side during the death of his mother, and must have been his father's best friend and pride and joy. He endured not only the death of his mother as a young teenager, but the separation from his young brothers Joseph and little Benjamin a year after his mother's death.

Almost a year after leaving Bangor, Seth Noble received the most dreaded news via Cape Ann (Sandy Bay/Rockport), Massachusetts. Seth Jr., age twenty-one, was reported lost at sea on a schooner bound for Boston. Found in the New Hampshire Historical Society in Concord, New Hampshire at the Tuck Library was the following article in the *New Hampshire Gazette* (Wednesday, October 31, 1798, p.3):

MELANCHOLLY [sic]

The Sch. Susannah, Capt. Daniel Jamison, was found on Saturday morning, the 20th inst. Between Holly-boat-Point and Sandy Bay, (Cape-Ann) wreck'd to pieces; she sailed from Penobscot on Wednesday previous, bound to Boston, and is supposed to have struck on a rock, many leagues from shore, overset, and filled in the bay, her sternpost and rudder not being found, and her foremast appearing to have been cut away; from the trunk, cloaths, and papers, which have been picked up it is supposed there were twenty persons on board who have probably all perished; nine days having elapsed since the shipwreck, and no accounts of the deliverance of any of them been received; no part of the boat or oars were discovered with the wreck; though it is probable had they taken to the boat, the gale must have proved destructive to them – the sea running very high, and the weather thick. The following articles were washed on shore, viz. Cloaths marked, S.H.-- H.P.—O.D. – R.T. – B. – Umbrellas, R. Hall; D. Jamison; a Gun Stock, W. Cordwell; a Hat, R.

Hall; a Chest of cloaths suppose to belong to **Mr. S. Noble, jr;** another chest of cloaths of Mr. B. Clap, and a box marked Joshua Bangs. The chests went on shore some hours after the vessel; this circumstance strengthens the opinion that the vessel was overset some considerable distance from shore.

This above newspaper article appeared with the same type font in many of the New England papers of the day including the *Boston Gazette, Columbian Centinel* (Boston), *Salem Gazette,* and *The Oracle of the Day* (Portsmouth, New Hampshire). (These early newspapers are on microprint at the Fogler Library at the University of Maine.) This shipwreck discovery is based on information obtained from the following entry in Rev. Seth Noble's diary:

Oct. 20, 1798. *O death! my son Seth lost at sea; and all who were with him; supposed to be at Boon Island. All in number who were lost was 26.*

Nov. 5. *Cool. Went to Ipswich, on my way to Sandy bay.*

Nov. 6. *Pleasant, went to sd. Bay; and got my poor son's clothes.*

Nov. 7. *Returned home with a heavy heart [2, p. 208].*

Mary Sibbalds, a dedicated volunteer at the Sandy Bay Historical Society in Rockport, Massachusetts, found a reference to this shipwreck in the extensive work of a young high school student, Paul Sherman. Mr. Sherman, in 1964, recorded the mention of the Schooner SUKEY* in *The Diary of Rev. William Bentley, D.D., Pastor of the East Church, Salem, Massachusetts, Volume 2, January, 1793 – December, 1802:*

p. 286,
Oct. 25, 1798 – *We have information that the Schooner SUKEY of Boston is actually lost near Sandy Bay, Cape Ann and all on board have perished..*

p. 287,
Oct. 27, 1798 – *We have the alarming report that the loss of the schooner SUKEY will probably prove the loss of many valuable lives and of many excellent women.*
p. 289,
Nov. 13, 1798 – *We have the melancholy list of the unfortunate sufferers in the SCH. SUSANNAH cast away off Cape Ann from Penobscot. There were 15 men on board & 5 ladies. Three of the ladies were of the family Hitchborn [47].*

*SUKEY is an old-fashioned nickname for Susannah and it suggests that its use speaks to a certain familiarity of this ship to the seafaring area. It was William Bentley's father, Joshua, who rowed Paul Revere across the Charles River on his famous ride into American history.

Recently discovered, in *The Oracle of the Day* (Portsmouth, New Hampshire) Saturday, October 27, 1798, p. 3, under Shipping News:

We hear that Sat. Night the Sch. SUKEY of Boston was wrecked on Sandy Bay, near Cape Ann and every soul on Board perished and that five of the bodies have since driven on shore.

This devastating loss of Seth Noble's firstborn son, Seth, Jr. was a loss which touched homes from Bangor to Boston and was one of the earliest known shipwrecks of a ship built and first launched in Bangor, Maine in 1793. The Searsport Marine Museum in Searsport, Maine shared with me the following information from "Sailing Vessels Built in the Penobscot River Towns in Maine" by Robert Applebee (1941) :

*The Schooner Susanna was registered in Penobscot at 90 (91/95) tons, 68' 0" x 20'9" x 7'6" Bill. Sq. and was Built in **Bangor** Me 1793.   John Lord, master '93*
Daniel Darling '95
Owners: John Lord, Boston; Robert Hichborn, Frankfort,1793; Philip Hichborn, Boston; Robert Hichborn, Prospect 1795[45]

Susanna is the name as it would appear on the vessel and its paperwork. This spelling is without the "h" on the end and very well may be the correct spelling, but all newspapers spell the vessel with an "h" and the schooner was named for Mrs. Susannah Hichborn, Robert Hichborn's wife, whose name was spelled with an "h."

Sch. means she is schooner rigged. A two masted schooner is assumed here because of her vintage and length.

Penobscot is her home port and this is the customhouse serving her homeport in what is today Castine. Even though Bangor was incorporated in 1791 and Castine was incorporated in 1796, these two names were not used in the newspaper articles. Penobscot was the old name still recognized by many in New England.

90 (91/95) tons is the calculated burthen of the vessel and was an international standard for calculating taxes, etc.

68' 0" x 20'9" x 7'6" are the dimensions used to calculate her burthen. 68' 0" is the length on deck; i.e., the distance between vertical perpendiculars and excludes forward overhang and any overhang of the main boom aft. 20'9" is the extreme breadth of the vessel (at the widest point), 7'6" is the depth of hold; i.e. from the deck to the keel (and not draught or draft; i.e., from the water line to the bottom of the keel, although depth of hold is a good approximation of draught).

Bill means she has a billet head; i.e., she did not have a figurehead.

Sq. means she has a square stern.

Built in Bangor, Me 1793 is self-explanatory and explodes the myth that she was built at Stockton Springs [46, p. 13; and 50, p. 101].

John Lord master 1793 and *Owners:* John Lord, Boston; Robert Hichborn, Frankfort, 1793; is information taken right off of the 1793 customs document.

Daniel Darling [Master] 1795 and [owners] Philip Hichborn, Boston; Robert Hichborn, Prospect, 1795; is information taken off the 1795 customhouse document. (Robert and Philip were brothers both born in Boston.)

Robert Hichborn, Frankfort, 1793; Robert Hichborn, Prospect; is the same person known as Robert Hichborn, Sr. then living at Fort Point (Cape Jellison, today Stockton Springs), father of Susan and Eliza Hichborn. Prospect was set off from Frankfort in 1794.

From the 1882, *History of Penobscot County Maine* is a section taken from Jacob McGaw's *Sketch of Bangor,* in the Maine Historical Society:

> *With its incorporation Bangor received a new impetus. Mr. [Robert] Treat had been successful in his traffic. From the poultry trade he derived enormous profits. His means were sufficient to enable him to go into the business of shipbuilding. He employed Mr. [William] Boyd as master-carpenter, and in 1791 laid the keel of a vessel, which in two years was ready to receive her rigging and sails. Mr. Treat had the opportunity to avail himself of the craft of Mr. Harlow for pumps and blocks; that of Mr. Timothy Crosby, son of Simon, for masts and spars; and that of Mr. Jacob Dennett for boats. This vessel was the first larger than a boat, ever built in the region of Bangor above Fort Point [51, p. 539].*

Even though the above description does not mention the name of the schooner built in 1793, it is clear that this is the Hichborn schooner – SUSANNAH. It was also reported that during the two years building of Bangor's first schooner, it was referred to as "the Treat ship" and was built and launched near the red bridge [1, p. 44]. The Hichborn schooners were known as packets and were made to haul lumber, fish, poultry, fruit, and butter to the Boston markets and carried passengers at the same time. Joseph Potter built lumber mills in 1786, and shingles were also made for the Boston market. The streams were filled with fish, and the quantity taken at this time would astound the fishermen of today. Seventy-five to one hundred barrels a day would be filled with shad and alewives, and forty salmon a day at Treat's Falls was an average day of fishing [51, p. 539].

1798 – 1805

The news of the wreck of the SUSANNAH affected the entire Penobscot River and Bay region. It was built and stocked in Bangor with goods for sale in Boston, and the many passengers who boarded this vessel came from Boston and the surrounding area of Bangor. Seth Noble may very well have watched the schooner being built. According to Jacob McGaw in his *Manuscript Sketch of Bangor,* this early shipyard was a short distance below the Penjejawock Stream [79, p.40] and thus not far from Seth Noble's home, near East Summer Street, Bangor. McGaw also stated that "this vessel made one or two voyages to Liverpool, England with cargoes of lumber and was then sold at Boston [79, p. 40]." The SUSANNAH was on its way to be sold in Boston at the time of the shipwreck.

The most important discovery made regarding this shipwreck is the passenger list I found printed in the *Salem Gazette* on microprint at the University of Maine Fogler Library in Orono, Maine. This passenger list, which was probably obtained by the ship's log washing up on shore, may be one of the earliest known passenger lists of a nautical disaster from the Penobscot Bay region. This list also sheds new light on the "dark ages" of Bangor history, namely the post-revolutionary war period of the late eighteenth century. The following recently discovered passenger list of this shipwreck adds further to our knowledge of the loss of life long since forgotten until now. In the Friday, November 16, 1798 *Salem Gazette* is the following:

Nov. 15,
We have ascertained that the unfortunate persons on board the Susannah, wrecked a short time since near Cape Ann, were, Capt. Daniel Jamison of Penobscot, Mr. Robert Treat, jun. do.,* Francis Haynes, do., Seth Noble, jun., do., Beriah Clap, do., J. Potter, do., Richard Hall, Medford, Jona. Brown, Cambridge, Joshua Bangs, Harwick, Oliver Deverix, Boston, Master John Pulling, do., Miss Susannah Hichborn, Penobscot, Miss Sarah Hichborn, do., Miss Eliza Hichborn, Boston, Miss Sarah Pulling, do., Mrs. S. Stevenson, do., and four other persons, whose names are unknown, – Neither Mr. Cordwell nor Mr. E. Bangs were among the passengers. –

Two of the persons whose names are undiscovered, are supposed to belong to some country town back of Boston; and the other two are conjectured to be seamen belonging to the vessel. [*A note to the reader – do = ditto.]

A known passenger, not mentioned on this list, was Sylvia Knapp, firstborn child of Samuel and Rachel (Grover) Knapp of (what is today) north Brewer. The family later removed to the town of Bradley. The Knapp family was originally from Mansfield, Massachusetts and therefore the mention, possibly of "some country town back of Boston."

Rev. Seth Noble preached on the succeeding Sabbath, November 11th (probably for the grieving families of the victims of the wreck of the SUSANNAH), from II Kings 4:26, where a woman prayed to God to seek relief from the overwhelming grief at the death of her son. God answered her plea by giving her child life everlasting:

Run now, I pray thee, to meet her, and say unto her, Is it well with thee? Is it well with thy husband? Is it well with thy child? And she answered, It is well [2, p. 208].

He was also reported to have given this eulogy at a later date in Bangor possibly in the following spring of 1799 [1, p. 50]. Alice V. Ellis, in her 1955, *The Story of Stockton Springs, Maine*, mentions a notation in the James Stower Journal and a reference to Rev. Seth Noble of Bangor delivering a sermon in what was then Prospect. I could conclude from this entry that Rev. Seth Noble gave his eulogy for the lost souls of the shipwreck of the SUSANNAH at the Robert Hichborn, Sr. mansion in Prospect (today Stockton Springs). No one suffered more than the Hichborn family with the loss of daughters Susan and Eliza and niece Sarah.

A trip to Cape Jellison, where the SUSANNAH last weighed anchor and sailed off into eternity, felt somewhat like "time travel." The large empty cellar is the only remnant of Robert and Susannah Hichborn's estate, very close to the Fort Point Light House (1835) and the former site of the 1759 Fort Pownal. Mindful of my recent discovery of this shipwreck, I felt compelled to find the cemetery where Robert Hichborn, Sr. is buried. Just before his death Robert Hichborn gave a part of his land for a cemetery for the early settlers. It was Robert Hichborn, Sr. who was the first to be buried in it. As I approached his broken carved headstone lying on the ground (it has recently been repaired after a phone call to the sexton), a family secret, lost in the cloud of time, was made abundantly clear to me. Robert Hichborn, Sr., father of Susannah (Susan) and Elizabeth (Eliza) died October 18, 1800; the exact day of the second anniversary of the shipwreck SUSANNAH.

The words written on his tombstone, beneath a beautifully carved schooner, seemed to be timeless, "His pain and sorrow are no more for he is now with his Lord." Also written on the back of his headstone are the words "One of the Historic Boston Tea Party." One could easily understand that sixty-year-old Robert Hichborn literally might have died of a broken heart. Mrs. Susannah (Ellingwood) Hichborn left their beautiful Maine estate after the death of her husband Robert, and she returned to Boston and is buried there.

The Robert Hichborn family of Cape Jellison (Stockton Springs) came to this area in 1785 from Boston and started building their large dwelling in 1791 [46, p. 7]. The basement of this estate can still be seen on the corner of the East Cape and Fort Point Roads. The Hitchborn (spelled Hichborn in Maine) family of Boston were close relatives of Paul Revere whose mother Deborah (Hitchborn) Revere was Robert Hitchborn, Sr's. aunt. Paul Revere and Robert Hitchborn were first cousins who grew up together and lived next door to each other in Boston [41]. Robert Hitchborn married Susannah Ellingwood in Boston on July 16, 1765, and had ten children. Their eldest child, Robert Hichborn, Jr., became Bangor's second town clerk, and many of his descendants are living in this area today. A very touching remembrance to the victims of this shipwreck is a letter written by Robert Hitchborn, Sr. to his cousin, Paul Revere:

[Prospect, District of Maine, January 4th 1799]

I received your very obliging letter which gave a degree of pleasure at this time it being a Time and Day of Trobel.

> *My dear friends the news whose so sudden and unexpected that my mind teuk ets flitz and never returned till it had ransacked the bottom of the Oshon from Cape Ann to Cape Cod and back down the Oshon Shor and over the face of the Great Waters after my dear daughters till it portadged my old body in such a manner that I was ardly abel to sleep about but live in hopes that the great Orther in dew time will now string the harp and cause me to partake of mercy as well as judgment that you and your dear friends and families may enjoy pece of mind is the wish of your friend and Brother*
>
> *Robert Hitchborn*
>
> *P.S. My respects to all friends my mind whont admit of polliticke. Let me hear from you as soon as posebel [41, p. 467].*

Although the above letter was written by a man whose English is less than perfect, it is supremely expressive of his enormous sorrow. When Robert Hichborn mentions "dear friends and families," this can be taken literally to convey his sorrow for the death of the children of the participants in Paul Revere's famous midnight ride on April 19, 1775 from Boston to Lexington (still celebrated as Patriots' day in Massachusetts and Maine), who were also aboard this ill-fated schooner. Miss Sarah Pulling and Master John Pulling are the children of John and Sarah Pulling of Boston. John Pulling is reputed to be the famous lantern hanger of the Old North Church of Boston or the "one if by land and two if by sea" fame, so beautifully portrayed in the Henry Wadsworth Longfellow poem, "Paul Revere's Ride," written in 1861.

This schooner went down with such famous firstborn sons and daughters of the American Revolution, that one might suppose that the British targeted it. From the description in the *New Hampshire Gazette*, it appears that the ship hit a rock and broke its stern post and filled with water. I could not find any mention of a storm at the time of the wreck, but the article mentioned "the gale must have proved destructive to them – the sea running very high and the weather thick." Did "thick weather" mean heavy fog or did the schooner go down in a fierce October snowstorm? Even today, late October weather on the coast of Maine is notoriously unpredictable and dangerous for sailing vessels.

The lifeboat or captain's boat was never found, and many circumstances can come to mind when one contemplates the horror aboard the sinking SUSANNAH. As her sternpost is broken and she rapidly starts to sink in the frigid waters and high seas off Cape Ann, is there any chance for the twenty passengers to even board the captain's boat? Even hearing this information over 200 years later, the horror is still palpable. The only aids to navigation in 1798 were the magnetic compass, a clock, a quadrant or sextant (useable in clear weather only), a lead line, a log line, and human ears and eyeballs.

It is Hichborn (spelled Hitchborn and Hitchbourne in early Boston records [41]) family oral history that many passengers were on their way to the wedding of twenty-four-year-old Susannah (Susan), who was to be wed in Boston [46, p. 13]. It is also noted that the intended came to Cape Ann and picked up her trunk with brass nail heads forming the initials "**S. H.**" on the lid in the waters off Cape Ann (Halibut-Point). (Further information regarding the passengers aboard the SUSANNAH can be found in Appendix 2.)

The death of Seth, Jr. affected Seth Noble in a way that would influence his decision to eventually pull up stakes on the east coast and make the dangerous trek west. Rev. Seth Noble preached in churches in East Kingston, Exeter, Kensington, Pittsfield, Rye, Salisbury, and Stratham, all in New Hampshire. Just prior to the death of Seth, Jr., he was also reported to have opened "singing schools" on December 25, 1797 in Newfield, Maine and January 5, 1798 in Lamper River, New Hampshire [2, p. 208].

He left New Market, New Hampshire on November 29, 1799 after residing there for two years. His youngest son John Adams Noble was born in New Market on April 18, 1799. He decided to return to the town of his birth, Westfield, Hampden County, Massachusetts. He lived with his relatives, probably on the Noble farm where he was born. He preached at Becket, Blandford, Feeding Hills, Ireland, Montgomery, Russell, and Springfield and then moved to Montgomery, Massachusetts on April 13, 1801. He was installed as their first pastor on November 4, 1801 at the age of fifty-eight. An interesting description of Rev. Mr. Noble was documented by Lucius Boltwood, in a 1876 letter from Rev. Elisha D. Barrett, who was born in Montgomery in 1790 and clearly remembered Rev. Seth Noble:

> *I can say that I well remember Rev. Seth Noble as the first pastor of Montgomery. He was tall and slim and rather good looking. He was active and energetic and his step was quick and firm and his gait graceful. He wore a white wig, which he used to powder. He was of a lively, social disposition and agreeable in his manners. As a man he was much respected and esteemed. I was too young at the time to be a competent judge of his scholarship, but to my youthful mind, he was a student. As a preacher he was sound and able. His sermons, I recollect, were well prepared, scholarly, unique, systematic, and evangelical. On one occasion, a child by the name of Bartholomew was killed by a falling tree, and Mr. Noble preached the funeral discourse over the open grave from Ecclesiastes 9:12.*
>> *[For man also knoweth not his time: as the fishes that are taken in an evil net, and as the birds that are caught in the snare; so are the sons of men snared in an evil time, when it falleth suddenly upon them.]*
>
> *The effect was electrical, and proved the most dramatic scene I have ever witnessed. I do not remember any difficulty between him and his people, as the cause of his removal. The society, I know was weak, and the salary must have been small, and raised with great difficulty. A claim, which he had upon land in Ohio, was I think, his inducement to remove to the state [2, p. 209].*

Rev. E. Barrett's sister, Mrs. Joanna Allyn also wrote that Rev. Mr. Noble was:

> *an excellent singer, and taught singing-schools in Montgomery, and also generally sang in church. I can even now hear his sweet voice [2, p. 209].*

In a letter dated September 22, 1801, Rev. Seth Noble noted that the salary offered him would be insufficient for the support of "even a small family." In October or November of 1805 **"O Death!"** visits Seth Noble once again. Ruhama his wife of twelve years died and was buried in Montgomery, Massachusetts. She is buried in the Pitcher Cemetery with the initials R. N. and the year of her death, 1805. She did not die in Montgomery, as the vital records do not show a record of her death. The vital records of Westfield do not exist for this time period, and it is quite possible that Ruhama died in the family home of Seth Noble in Westfield, and then she was buried in Montgomery where they resided.

It is not known if Seth was with Ruhama at the time of her death. It is around this time that Seth had secured his land within the "Refugee Tract" in Ohio. It is quite possible that he made a visit to "the Ohio Promised Land" on the western frontier, in 1805. Ruhama's death was a sign for him to continue his part in the fulfillment of his earlier vision of the promise of America and his dream of the great American Reformation. He, like many others, was struck with "Ohio Fever!"

Chapter Seven

1805 – 1807

Ohio
A Pilgrimage for the Promise of America

✝✝✝

That a new America was steadily taking form beyond the Appalachians was one of the clearest signs of the times. Down the same road as John Adams traveled . . . came small caravans . . . – families with children and household belongings piled onto heavy wagons, bound for Ohio, a journey of more than 700 miles.

---- David McCullough,
JOHN ADAMS

Congress did, indeed, appropriate lands under the denomination of "Soldier lands," in Ohio, but no care was taken that the soldiers should get them. The soldiers were ignorant of the ways and means to obtain their bounty lands and there was no one appointed to inform them.

---- Joseph Plumb Martin,
Being A Narrative of . . . a Revolutionary Soldier . . .
1830 (Stockton Springs) Maine

It was represented that the lands in Ohio . . . were rich, the climate mild, and the summers long; and that breadstuffs and other articles of food there, were abundant and cheap. . . . nothing could break the [Ohio] spell.

---- William D. Williamson,
History of the State of Maine (1832)

★★★★★★★★★★★★★

Rev. Seth Noble

From *A Short History of Ohio Land Grants,* compiled by State Auditor, State of Ohio:

In 1798, Congress directed the Secretary of War to insert notices in newspapers in New York, Pennsylvania, Massachusetts, Vermont and New Hampshire inviting Canadian refugees to apply for and file claims for land. Claimants were required to show that they had been forced to flee their homes there because of aid they gave to the colonists [57].

Today, downtown Columbus, Ohio, between Mound and Main Streets marks the land and log cabin of Rev. Seth Noble with a sign proclaiming **"NOBLE ST."** In a document signed on February 13, 1802, by President Thomas Jefferson and Secretary of State James Madison pursuant to the 1801 act of Congress entitled *An Act Regulating the Grants of Land Appropriated for the Refugees for the British Provinces of Canada and Nova Scotia,* Seth Noble was granted two tracts of land containing a total of six hundred and forty acres (lots # 13 and 32 from the Refugee Land Survey Map of 1801). It was located in the then town of Franklinton, (today Columbus), near the site of the present Franklin County Hall of Justice.

What would make a man who is in his sixties, widowed with seven children from twenty-two to six years of age, decide to make the arduous journey from Montgomery, Massachusetts to the wilderness of Ohio? The quote from Elisha D. Barrett, who remembered Rev. Seth Noble from his last congregation in Montgomery, states that the congregation was poor and he did not "remember any difficulty between him and his people, as the cause of his removal [to Ohio] [2, p. 209]."

Many veterans were granted land in Ohio, but very few actually went there to settle. Both Jonathan Eddy and John Allan were granted parcels of land in the same area as Seth Noble, but neither made claims on their land. The heirs of John Allan, in 1824, failed to recover John Allan's land (lot # 25) in a lawsuit based upon technical grounds [55, p. 511]. Joseph Plumb Martin who moved to Prospect (today Stockton Springs), Maine sold his bounty land in Ohio (100 acres) to Daniel Aiken for a very small sum of money [59, p. xiv].

After the death of his wife Ruhama in 1805, the offer of free fertile land in the Northwest Territory of Ohio restored Seth Noble's unrequited patriotic fervor of yore. He could not relinquish his dream of the fulfillment of God's "Promised Land" and the "great American Reformation." Since the dream had not yet been fulfilled, only personal sacrifice in the form of a pilgrimage could help settle the great Northwest Territory and thereby sow the seeds for a future America ordained by God.

An added bonus to his decision was the farmer's dream of choice fertile land, with the renewal of his youthful excitement of being able to bring the word of God to yet another new frontier. This was inducement enough to follow his dream of founding a church along the Scioto River in the future capital of Ohio. This dream had been painfully denied him along the banks of the Penobscot River in Bangor.

Even with all of the luxuries of twenty-first century travel, I would not look forward to driving to Ohio from New England. So what was it like for Seth Noble to make this journey in the early nineteenth century? From the *History of Columbus Centennial Celebration,* by Stephen Fitzpatrick in 1897:

> *It is probable that when Franklin County was created in 1803 by the first general assembly of Ohio, Franklinton had a population of fifty or more. It was in Columbus that the courts of the county were established and Lucas Sullivant was made clerk of the court. Lucas Sullivant was the prime mover in this county and built his home there in 1801.*

With Kentucky becoming a state in 1792 and Tennessee in 1796, the expansion westward was now in full swing. Although Kentucky and Tennessee were a result of southern expansion of Virginia and the Carolina regions, Ohio was the first state to be created from the public domain. Even though the early stream of Ohio settlers were mainly American born, there were Yankee Puritans meeting Southerners, Dutch descendants from New York clearing land nearby the Scotch Irish descendants of Northern

Ireland, Quakers living next to Maryland Episcopalians, and Carolina Huguenots were wondering how to converse with Pennsylvanian Germans. One might even go so far as to say that the future melting pot of America began in earnest in Ohio.

In 1798, George and Felix Renick, of Irish descent but born and raised in Virginia, heard about the beauty and fertility of the western lands. They set out on horseback from Virginia and arrived at Marietta, where they obtained maps at the land office run by General Rufus Putnam. They made their way to the town of Franklinton (Columbus) and they described the following:

> *... considerable number of log cabins, most of which had recently been put up and were without chinking, daubing or doors [43, p. 219].*

After the Renick brothers rested in Franklinton for a few days, they proceeded down the Scioto River to the Ohio River Valley to return to Virginia. In May of 1801 Felix Renick returned to Chillicothe on the Scioto River to purchase a large tract of land at $2.50 per acre. This land was later to become Indian Creek farm [43, p. 220].

Margaret van Horn wrote about her arduous journey to Ohio in 1810. This ordeal was so horrible, she knew she would have to spend the rest of her life in this new land, as a return trip would be unthinkable [54].

In the spring of 1805 the Renick brothers drove 68 head of corn-fattened cattle overland from the Scioto River Valley to Baltimore, arrived safely and sold the entire herd at thirty-two dollars per head. Rev. Seth Noble set out for Ohio sometime between 1805 and 1806. Seth Noble was no stranger to the canoe, so I had assumed he would have ventured down Lake Erie to Cleveland and taken an Indian trail to Franklinton. The Franklin County Genealogical and Historical Society in Columbus spent much time trying to obtain information for me on Rev. Mr. Noble and this early period in Columbus history. From a letter written to me on March 23, 2004, by researcher Susan Bauer:

> *Transportation in the decade was either by boat (flatboat or canoe) or on Indian trails. The Scioto River was*

supposedly navigable up to Franklinton from the Ohio River. Every major stream had Indian paths on one or both banks. The major streams in central Ohio flow south and the land is mostly flat. The east bank of the Scioto had a major trail that extended north along Whetstone (now Olentangy River) to Worthington (founded in 1803) and eventually to Lake Erie. There were also some trails that went east/west, such as the one connection Zanesville, Newark, Granville, Worthington and Dublin. Travelers could get to this trail via the Muskingum River from the Ohio River. This is the trail that the founder of Worthington took in 1802/03. If Seth Noble came south from the Cleveland area, he may have traveled on the Walhonding Indian trail that went by Coshocton and Mt. Vernon and entered the central Ohio region at a southwest angle. . . .

In *The History of Madison County, Ohio*, written in 1883, is the only mention of the arrival of Seth Noble in Ohio and the building of his log cabin. His grandson, Mr. Albert Bartholomew, of Detroit, Michigan (son of Martin and Sarah Noble Bartholomew) reported that his grandfather's log cabin was still in existence in 1853:

In the spring of 1806, my grandfather came to Ohio and settled in Franklinton. He built a house on his land and I recognized it in 1853 when I visited Columbus [9].

In the records of the Franklinton County Genealogical and Historical Society is a mention of Seth Noble giving son-in-law Martin Bartholomew half of his Lot 32 (150 acres). Martin and Sarah (Noble) Bartholomew more than likely followed Seth to Ohio in 1807, and he gave them the land adjoining his farm. They appeared to have paid the taxes on this property until 1817 as reported in *The Old Northwest Genealogical Quarterly* (Vol. 15, p.128). Sarah and Martin returned to Montgomery, Massachusetts in 1808.

The following reference is an interesting introduction of Seth Noble's arrival in Franklinton, from the *Old Northwest Genealogical Quarterly* of April, 1907 by H. Warren Phelps:

The Reverend Seth Noble, generally known as Parson Noble, who came from Montgomery near Westfield, Massachusetts, and settled upon lands at Franklinton where Columbus west of the river now is, first came to the home of Edward Phelps in 1806 when on his way to find the lands for which he had a Refugee Grant from the United States Government, and was a frequent visitor there, and preached at the Phelps' cabin. . . .

Rev. Seth Noble's first recorded sermon preached in Ohio was at the J. Andrus cabin in Worthington on April 9, 1806 [9, p. 1027]. William Morrow Beach, M.D., grandson of Seth Noble and son of Uri and Hannah (Noble) Beach wrote a wonderful family biography of the Beach family and his grandfather, Rev. Seth Noble. He quotes dates and places of different sermons delivered by his grandfather; one can only assume that his book of sermons was given to him by his mother, Hannah Noble, daughter of Rev. Seth and Hannah (Barker) Noble; she seemed to have remained in Montgomery, and married Nathan Gorham in 1807. They both came to Worthington in 1812 with their two daughters, Elizabeth and Belinda, and possibly Seth and Ruhama's youngest son, John Adams Noble, age seven. Nathan Gorham was killed in a sawmill accident in 1814, thus leaving Hannah, age twenty-five, widowed with the care of three children.

Uri Beach was one of twelve children of Elizabeth (Kilbourn) and Obil Beach of Poultney, Vermont and was the first of his family to move to Ohio in 1814; the words of his son William Morrow Beach are worth repeating:

In the year 1812, my father, Uri Beach, was 23 years of age and was determined to emigrate to Ohio. He met with great opposition from the family; but he arranged his "pack," and swinging it over his shoulder, started alone and on foot. He came first to Cleveland, near where he stopped for three days to replenish his purse by working.

He worked for three days for a farmer, in helping to build a mill-dam, where he had to work all the time in water sometimes waist-deep. For this he received $1 a day; but as he had to pay the tavern keeper 75 cents a day for his board, he found he was only 75 cents better off for his three days hard work. He then struck a "bee-line" for Marietta, Ohio, which had then been settled for 24 years. There he made 4 barrels of cider, for a farmer, on the halves; and taking his two barrels down to Marietta, sold it out of his skiff, at a lively rate to the United States soldiers quartered there, at 12½ cents a quart. Returning up the river with his skiff, he washed out of the pumice, at the cider mill, about three pecks of apple seed, which, adding to the weight of his original pack, he swung over his shoulder and took another bee-line for Worthington, Ohio directing his course through the wilderness as he best could, and strapping himself in the tops of trees at night to save himself from being devoured by wolves while trying to obtain his needed rest. In the spring of 1813, he rented a small piece of ground at Worthington and planted a part of his apple seeds for a nursery. In the spring of 1814, he came to Madison County and bought 92 acres of land in Darby Township from Walter and Ann May Dun and planted more apple seeds. He married Mrs. Hannah (Noble) Gorham on September 1, 1816. They are both buried in Amity, Ohio [9, p. 1073].

This above oral history of William Morrow Beach, M.D. was a real treasure to find in the 1883 *History of Madison County, Ohio* [9]. Dr. Beach also recorded the dates and places of sermons of Rev. Seth Noble, the grandfather who died before he was born. Dr. Beach wrote that our Rev. Mr. Noble preached at Granville, Licking County, Ohio, August 17, 1806; at Franklinton, August 24, 1806; and at Derby (Big Darby), September 22, 1806.

Recorded in the vital records of the Ohio Archives and now available at the genealogical records of Early Ohio Settlers, 1700s-1900s, is the third marriage of Rev. Seth Noble to the widow Mrs. Margaret (Mary) Riddle on December 3, 1806 in Franklinton

Township by the Justice of the Peace, James Kilbourn. Regarding Mrs. Riddle, Lucius Boltwood, reported:

> *In the vicinity of Franklinton, Ohio were many, in 1807, who had previously resided in and about Maugerville, Nova Scotia. She is thought by some of the grandchildren of Rev. Seth Noble, to have been one of these [2, p. 211].*

Remember the story of Seth Noble's harrowing escape from the British in Maugerville while hiding under the bed of Mrs. Wasson's daughter? I tried to learn the identity of Margaret (Mary) Riddle and whether she was a member of his congregation in Maugerville. A full search was commenced; since no records are available from that time in Maugerville, my vivid imagination is all that is left.

This book is meant to be a serious documented history of the time period and the life of Rev. Seth Noble, so I dare not proceed with my mindless wanderings, however . . . what if Margaret was the fourteen-year-old girl who hid him under her bed and rowed him across the river to safety, never to be seen again until twenty-nine years later, when their paths crossed on their way to Ohio? I apologize for this deviation from fact, but my sixth sense has been a great help in finding "bread crumbs" left to me by Seth Noble in a surprising paper trail. My imaginary story of Mrs. Riddle is all I have to share with the reader. It would be unusual for Mrs. Riddle to make the trip to Ohio alone, so perhaps her husband died along the way or shortly after she arrived. Did she make the journey to Ohio with Seth Noble? His grandchildren reported that they knew each other in Maugerville. No record was ever found of a Mr. Riddle or Mr. Magill Riddle being granted land in Ohio, so this part of Seth's final chapter will have to remain a mystery.

What is known about Mrs. Riddle is that she and Seth had only a very short time together after they married. Rev. Noble's cabin was on the land issued to Revolutionary War refugees from Nova Scotia (New Brunswick today) who sided with the colonists. This land was known as the Refugee Tract. It was on the current site of the Franklin County Hall of Justice. Today there is still a road called Refugee Road, which follows the southern boundary of the Refugee Tract across Franklin and Fairfield counties.

The original grant of land was surveyed in 1801 and Seth Noble would have been the "next door" neighbor of his old Revolutionary War "buddies" Jonathan Eddy and John Allan, had they decided to take on the arduous journey to Ohio. It was reported that the descendants of Jonathan Eddy and John Allan had great difficulty obtaining any financial compensation for their fathers' lands.

Lucius M. Boltwood stated that:

No Congregational or Presbyterian clergyman is believed to have previously held regular service nearer than Marietta, in that part of Ohio prior to Seth Noble [2, p.219].

Also reported in the *Old Northwest Genealogical Quarterly*, of April 1907 by H. Warren Phelps was a fall meeting in Chillicothe, Ohio:

October 1806
Rev. Seth Noble, a minister of the Congregational Church, lately from the State of Massachusetts, appeared before the Presbytery and presented a certificate of his regular standing as a minister of the gospel, in that church, and stated to Presbytery that other papers, more fully exhibiting his regular introduction to the gospel ministry, and good standing as a laborer in the Lord's Vineyard, are coming forward with his family, whereupon the Presbytery cheerfully admitted the Rev. Seth Noble to preach the gospel. . . . The Presbytery unanimously agreed to invite Mr. Noble to a seat, as a corresponding member, who took his seat accordingly . . . [History of Chillicothe Presbytery].

On August 9, 1807, it was reported that Rev. Seth Noble preached his last sermon in Franklinton, from Matthew 11:28,

Come unto me, all ye that labour and are heavy laden, and I will give you rest.

Rev. Seth Noble

The Franklinton Historical Society sent me an article by John Switzer for the *Columbus Metro Dispatch*, Sunday March 14, 2004, mourning the loss of a local landmark. A sadly common story these days, he lamented the loss of the beautiful 1801 grand home of Franklinton's founding father, Lucas Sullivant, which was being demolished in 1965 to make way for a car dealership. He felt sad every time he drove by the spot which now has a boulder monument marking the site of the first brick house in Franklinton. Seth Noble very likely concluded his lifelong religious service by offering a prayer to God in the very home, which John Switzer was rightfully lamenting.

In September of 1807, it was reported in the Franklinton vital records that a Miss Sophia Riddle died of consumption [2, p. 211]. Lucius Boltwood assumed this was the daughter of Seth Noble's wife, Mary (Riddle) Noble and one can presume she died of untreated progressive tuberculosis. It has been recorded that Rev. Seth Noble died in his log cabin in Franklinton (today downtown Columbus), on September 15, 1807 at the age of sixty-four [2, p. 211]. One could surmise that Seth Noble's last sermon was given as a farewell to his congregation, as he might have been suffering from the effects of tuberculosis on the linings of the heart and heart muscle. From my father's old 1949 medical book, *Diseases of the Heart*, by Charles K. Friedberg, M.D.,

> *Tuberculosis may be associated with extensive pulmonary changes causing increased pulmonary vascular resistance, pulmonary hypertension and cor pulmonale.*

What this means is that Seth Noble might have suffered from complications of tuberculosis which progressed over a period of time until this condition caused heart failure. My picture of the last days of Seth Noble is vivid in my imagination, but we can only guess what happened, since so very little has been recorded.

Did this Noble man have time to look back over his life and receive comfort from the memory of a life so fully lived? From Luke 4:24:

> *And he said, Verily I say unto you, No prophet is accepted in his own country.*

Until recently, neither Bangor nor Columbus had honored his contributions to the founding of their cities. The former research director of the Franklin County Historical Society, Gilbert F. Dodds once stated in *By One Spirit: Presbyterianism and the Formative Years (1806-1843)*:

> *Reverend Seth Noble must be considered as one of the pioneer preachers and founders in Franklin County, and it is very unfortunate that no monument or marker of any kind points to his last resting-place.*

After Mr. Dodds wrote the above words, the city of Columbus gave Seth a headstone and honored his contribution to the founding of Columbus with a large bronze marker. I could reiterate Mr. Dodds's statement with respect to the city of Bangor, as no marker, monument, park, or street exists today in Bangor to honor his sacrifices made for the founding and naming of this great city. Oddly enough, Seth is best remembered in Canada, where his rebel stands and support for the formation of America have been well documented.

At the time of his own death, I can imagine that his belief in a life lived in faith and love of God must have filled him with the joy of his eventual celestial reunion with his beloved "Sophronia" and firstborn son, Seth, Jr. He knew that he would never see the fulfillment of his promise of America, but was, instead, a pilgrim on earth for its formation. One price he paid for this sacrifice was his early separation from his two young sons, Joseph and Benjamin, whom he brought to Canada in desperation to be raised by his in-laws.

What did his entire earthly struggle really mean to him in the end? I believe that Seth Noble wholeheartedly gave himself to his Lord and died in peace and serenity. He was a poor farmer's son, who became a preacher, and as a young man he passionately took the road less traveled. He believed in the divine promise of America before it was popular. He publicly called for the independence of America from Great Britain and shouldered a musket in defense of his beliefs. As a result of his Revolutionary

War struggles for Maine he has been recorded to have been one of the most prominent men in securing Eastern Maine intact for the United States of America. He not only named Bangor and probably Hampden, Maine; he was the first minister to Maugerville (Sunbury County), Bangor (Brewer, Orrington, Holden, Eddington, Hampden and Orono), Montgomery, Massachusetts and Franklinton (Columbus), Ohio.

Seth died intestate and his children received only a pittance for his farm, which would today be prime real estate in the middle of Columbus. From the Chillicothe Supporter, April 21, 1810:

Noble, Seth died intestate. Heirs mentioned are Betsey Philips, wife of James, John Adams Noble, Joseph Noble, and Benjamin Noble, both residents of Nova Scotia, Hannah Gorham, wife of Benjamin Gorham, Sarah Bartholomew, wife of Martin Bartholomew [late Noble?], Mary Noble, resident of the state.

A photo taken by Hannah (Noble) (Gorham) Beach descendant, R. W. Parrott, and shared with me by John J. Noble, speaks volumes of the true importance of Seth Noble. A large obelisk marker for Seth's daughter Hannah, who was born in Bangor in 1789 and died in Amity, Ohio in 1854, is inscribed in large bold letters, "HANNAH – Consort of URI BEACH & Daughter of Rev. SETH NOBLE." What a touching tribute to her father! Mrs. Mary (Riddle) Noble died shortly after her husband, and it is not known where she is buried. She could have been buried next to her husband, but no records exist.

For many years there was no marker recognizing Seth Noble's grave in the Old Franklinton Cemetery in downtown Columbus between Souder Avenue and River Street. Today there is a marker for Seth Noble placed somewhere near his grave in the late twentieth century by the Franklinton Historical Society. He was one of four veterans honored with a Government Issue granite tombstone, which reads as follows:

1805 – 1807

```
SETH
NOBLE

MASS MILITIA
REV WAR
APR 15, 1743
SEP 15, 1807
```

Postscript: The discovery of Seth Noble's gravesite.

While researching Seth Noble's life in Ohio, I felt it was imperative to locate his grave. I contacted Lolita Guthrie of the Ohio Genealogical Society in Mansfield, Ohio. She commenced a complete search to find Seth Noble's final resting-place. She was having no luck until an amazing coincidence took place around the time of the 4th of July.

By chance or providence, Ms. Guthrie read an article in the *Columbus Dispatch* on July 1, 2003, "Historic Marker Missing from the Old Franklinton Cemetery." It was reported that local historian Bea Murphy informed City Attorney, Rick Pfeiffer, that the large bronze marker placed there in 1962 at the entrance to this historic graveyard had been stolen. In this article a mention was made of Seth Noble, a soldier of the Revolution. It seemed as if Seth Noble had jumped into the newspaper so that we could find him. Bea Murphy and John J. Noble kindly shared with me an old photo of the beautiful bronze marker:

OLD FRANKLINTON CEMETERY

This ancient burial ground of Central Ohio was established in a bend of the Scioto River in 1799 and is known as the "Old Franklinton Cemetery." The pioneers buried here are about one hundred in number. Seventy-one graves are marked largely by sandstone slabs, many having elaborately carved drawings and quaint inscriptions. Here also buried at least one soldier of the American Revolution, Reverend Seth Noble, first minister of the frontier town. In 1811, the first church in the community, Presbyterian, was erected by Lucas Sullivant, the founder of Franklinton, upon the present burial grounds. Sullivant himself was buried here in 1824, but his remains were removed to Green Lawn Cemetery years later.

In 1931, the West Side Board of Trade erected a granite obelisk monument in the center of the cemetery twenty-six feet in height. The memorial contains two commemorative tablets, one of which reads "In the Churchyard Stood the First Church of the Community – Built and Presented to the Congregation by Lucas Sullivant in 1811.

The strange, unknown people who built the ancient mounds and works knew the attractions and worth of this favored Scioto Valley.

The Franklinton Historical Society replaced this original 1962 bronze marker in 2005.

In *Generations, The Journal of the New Brunswick Genealogical Society* (Summer 2007), John Wood ended his biographical sketch of Rev. Seth Noble with, "It is therefore fortunate for us and an honour to his memory that, following his time on this stage, his voice can still be faintly heard." Since the eulogy given at Seth Noble's burial is unknown, I think it also appropriate to end this journey with the eulogy Rev. Seth Noble gave in Bangor for his dear Hannah in June 1790:

> **These all died in faith, not having received the promises, but having seen them afar off, and were persuaded of them, and embraced them, and confessed that they were strangers and pilgrims on the earth.**
>
> **Hebrews 11:13**

Appendix 1

The BANGOR TUNE by William Tans'ur (1706-1783)

In order to understand the music of Rev. Seth Noble's day we must first understand that, while the songs and hymns of today are more or less permanent marriages of poetry and music, the hymns of this period were divorced from the tunes, and would be mixed and matched to suit the occasion. The BANGOR TUNE was first published 1734 in London by William Tans'ur (Tanzer), *A Compleat Melody or The Harmony of Zion* (including other tunes honoring British Isle place names, e.g., St. David's, Dorchester, Dunchurch, Falmouth, Guilford, Newbury, St. Neot's, Mansfield, etc.). The BANGOR TUNE was originally set to Psalm 11 and entitled, "Bangor Tune – Composed in Three Parts."

The reference to "Three Parts" means that this tune was designed as a fugue for three different voices or instruments. One part starts, the second part is developed contrapuntually, and then the third in a strict order to all blend together. Just think of "row, row, row your boat gently down the stream," and how as children we sang this in three different parts until it all came together. Not to compare the BANGOR TUNE with "row, row, row your boat," but I hope this makes some sense to the reader. The original BANGOR TUNE was set to:

Psalm 11
To the Chief Musician, A Psalm of David

In the Lord put I my trust; how say ye to my soul,
Flee as a bird to your mountain?

For, lo, the wicked bend their bow, they make ready
their arrow upon the string, that they may
privily shoot at the upright in heart.

Appendix 1

If the foundations be destroyed, what can the righteous do?

The Lord is in his holy temple, the Lord's throne is in heaven: his eyes behold, his eyelids try, the children of men.

The Lord trieth the righteous: but the wicked and him that loveth violence his soul hateth.

Upon the wicked he shall rain snares, fire and brimstone, and a horrible tempest: this shall be the portion of their cup.

For the righteous Lord Loveth righteousness: his Countenance doth behold the upright.

Paul Revere and Josiah Flagg put together their favorite tunes in 1764 and called it *A Collection of the Best Psalm Tunes*. Paul Revere did the engraving and Josiah Flagg printed and published it in Boston. Revere and Flagg wrote in the preface to this publication:

He [the editor] has taken from every Author he has seen a few Tunes, which he judges to be the best. . . . That however we are oblig'd to the other Side of the Atlantick chiefly, for our Tunes, the Paper on which they are printed is the manufacture of our own Country [28].

This publication shows that the popularity of the BANGOR TUNE qualified it for an early Bostonian version of our current "Top 10 List" of popular songs. To even further confirm its appeal, 107 tunes, hymns and anthems by William Tans'ur were printed in 1771 in Newburyport, Massachusetts by Daniel Bayley under the title, *American Harmony: or Royal Melody Complete – in Two Volumes*. Seth Noble was living in Newburyport around this time and this is most likely the sheet music he would have used. The BANGOR TUNE was also very popular in Scotland and has been mistakenly called a Scottish psalm tune. This may

BANGOR TUNE

well have been performed with bagpipes and was so popular that Robert Burns mentioned it in his famous poem, "The Ordination:"

> *Mak haste an'turn King David owre,*
> *An' lilt wi' holy clangor;*
> *O' double verse come gie us four,*
> *An' skirl up the **Bangor***

There is also an unsubstantiated mention of the hymn tune BANGOR being performed at the funeral service for President George Washington in 1799. Since I have been unable to confirm this in any of the extensive writings on the life of our first president, I mention this only because it might be true.

From the *Hymnal Companion to the Lutheran Book of Worship,* by Marilyn Kay Stulken, Fortress Press, Philadelphia, 1981:

William Tans'ur was born in Dunchurch, Warwickshire, England and was baptized November 6, 1706. His parents were German with the name Tanzer, and it was William who changed the spelling of his name to Tans'ur. He was the son of a laborer and he became an itinerant musician, going from town to town teaching music and psalmody, playing the organ, and collecting materials for his book of psalm tunes and anthems. Eventually he settled in St. Neots [England] as a book seller and music teacher. He died in St. Neots on October 7, 1783 [32].

Professor Wyn Thomas of the School of Music at the University of Wales, Bangor, wrote in a letter on March 6, 2003:

The hymn-tune BANGOR is not a Welsh hymn-tune even though it has the name "Bangor" as a title. It does not appear in any of the Welsh language hymnals and is rarely sung even amongst English-speaking congregations.

William Tans'ur might well have been inspired to give it the name BANGOR:

a. because he visited our city en-route to Ireland (Bangor, Wales is 27 miles from Holyhead port)
b. because he visited the picturesque St. Deiniol's Cathedral in Bangor [Wales]
c. because he visited the picturesque Snowdonia mountain range (six miles from Bangor)
d. because he worked and trained at the St. Deiniol's Cathedral choir. Bangor has a long musical tradition that extends as far back as the 12th century and a very famous music manuscript collection called the "Bangor Pontifical" consisting of early chants and liturgical settings.

Etymology experts here at the University confirm that the name "Bangor" means "wooden (wattle) fence" but also refers to the – "gor" (BanGOR) or "cor" (the unmutated form of the word) which is the Welsh word for "choir" (Latin – "chorus" etc.). I have tried to find any written record of William Tans'ur's visit to our city of Bangor, but have been unable to do so.

When Seth Noble sang the hymn BANGOR, what words did he use? A short answer to this is, "we have no idea." A more accurate explanation is that the words to various hymn tunes during this time period were often chosen for the occasion. Dr. Isaac Watts (1674-1748) printed his "Psalms" in Boston in 1741 and Benjamin Franklin in Philadelphia also printed them. Because Dr. Watts wrote many versions of the psalms in common meter (C.M.) form, there was a demand for tunes written in common meter. Common meter contains four lines, the first, second, and fourth with six syllables, the third with eight.

Seth Noble has been the brunt of many light-hearted remarks and among them was a reference to his choice of the hymn BANGOR with such depressing or "doleful" words. From *A Dictionary of Hymnology,* ed. By John Julian, London, 1907, "Hark for the tombs a doleful sound," was used for burial hymns from the Baptist Praise book of 1871 [30]. An article in the *Bangor Daily News,* "City Named for Old Hymn" (Thursday,

Feb. 12, 1959), implies that the following words were the lyrics to the old hymn tune BANGOR:

Isaac Watts, D. D., HYMNS AND SPIRITUAL SONGS, Printed by Manning and Loring, Boston, 1769

Hymn 63 – Common Metre
A funeral thought.

Hark! From the tomb a doleful sound;
My ears attend the cry.
Ye living men, come view the ground
Where you must shortly lie.

Princes, this clay must be your bed,
In spite of all your towers;
The tall, the wise, the reverend head,
Must lie as low as ours.

Great, God! Is this our certain doom?
And are we still secure?
Still walking downward to the tomb,
And yet prepare no more.

Grant us, the power of quickening grace
To fit our souls to fly;
Then when we drop this dying flesh,
We'll rise above the sky [26].

In a letter from Mary Louise VanDyke (Librarian/Coordinator, of the Dictionary of American Hymnology, Oberlin College Librarian, Oberlin, Ohio), she listed 13 different collections of hymns published in America before 1791 from which Rev. Mr. Noble could have sung the above words and many others. If we could go back in time and listen to the Reverend Mr. Noble's congregation singing this hymn tune, I would expect that different words might have been used depending on the occasion.

A very clear example of how these hymns were actually sung is beautifully performed in the 1997 PBS special, "A Midwife's

Tale" (based on the Pulitzer Prize winning book by Laurel Thatcher Ulrich). These acappella voices seem to be singing to God with both praise and sorrow in a manner of allowing their souls to touch the heavens as an offering. The power and spiritual appeal of a choir of voices praying to God may not be appreciated today in a world of surround-sound, but in the unimaginably difficult lives of our early American ancestors, hymns were a new means of communicating with God. The above words were obviously intended for a funeral service and these might very well have been sung at the service for Seth Noble's wife Hannah, who died while he was away in Boston to secure the name Bangor for the future Queen City.

Professor Wyn Thomas School of Music, University of Wales, Bangor) may well have given us another idea on the hymn BANGOR, when he wrote to me that

William Tans'ur did his best to improve singing wherever he went and has been looked upon as the founder of community singing.

Seth Noble was reported to have had one of the best singing voices in the District of Maine [7]. The reader may recall that his former parishioner, Mrs. Allyn, wrote that, "I can even now, hear his sweet voice [2, p. 209]." Music was an important part of Rev. Seth Noble's life. He gave singing lessons wherever he traveled. Instead of viewing the hymn tune BANGOR as being ancient, it may very well have been part of a new wave of religious teachings. **William Tans'ur's principles of community singing as a gathering together of voices to invite God into one's heart and soul may well have inspired Seth Noble's love of music as an integral part of his ministry.**

During the September 22, 2003 incorporation presentation ceremony at the Bangor City Hall, when Seth Noble's descendant, Joanne Schotthoefer, performed the BANGOR TUNE, the words chosen for this occasion could have been sung by Seth Noble himself.

Hymn 20 – Common Meter
by Dr. Isaac Watts (1674-1748)

BANGOR TUNE

***The Provisions for the table of our Lord; or the
Tree of life, and river of love.***

1. LORD, we adore thy bounteous hand,
   And sing the solemn feast,

   Where sweet celestial dainties stand
   For every willing guest.

2. The tree of life adorns the board
   With rich immortal fruit,

   An ne'er an angry flaming sword
   To guard the passage to't,

3. The cup stands crown'd with living juice:
   The fountain flows above,

   And runs down streaming, for our use,
   In rivulets of love.

4. The food's prepar'd by heavenly art;
   The pleasure's well refin'd;

   They spread new life through every heart.
   And cheer the drooping mind.

5. Shout and proclaim the Saviour's love,
   Ye saints, that taste his wine;

   Join with our kindred saints above,
   In loud hosannas join.

6. A thousand glories to the God
   Who gives such joy as this.

Bangor, Wales is the site of the rectory dedicated to St. Deinol, the Abbot of Bangor. It is celebrated as being the site of the earliest British Christian monastery and was recorded to have housed over 2000 monks. By earliest accounts, Bangor, Wales established this monastery or college "for the instruction of youth" in 525 A.D. by a son of the Abbot of Bangor [23]. Is it possible that Rev. Seth Noble also chose the name Bangor as a vision of what he dreamed his new community might also become?

Whatever the reason Seth Noble chose the name of a spiritual tune, one can only marvel at the irony of this choice. Bangor, Maine is currently experiencing a revival of our once great Penobscot River, with the musical heritage of our nation being celebrated every summer in the form of the "American Folk Festival on the Bangor Waterfront."

With the summertime sounds of music now gracing our once famous riverfront, I find myself looking out over the water and can almost imagine a vision of our Rev. Seth Noble, in his white powdered wig and clerical bands, paddling his canoe past the festivities. Even though the BANGOR TUNE has long since been forgotten, music is still a centerpiece of the Queen City. Here's hoping that one day the city of Bangor, Maine will also embrace a revival of this early spiritual musical form and allow us to hear the beautiful sounds, for which Rev. Seth Noble named this city!

Appendix 2

Passengers Aboard The Shipwreck of the Schooner SUSANNAH Lost At Sea

Bangor – Boston, October 18, 1798

Off the Coast of Cape Ann, Massachusetts

The SUSANNAH was the first schooner built in Bangor and was launched in 1793 [45] at the Robert Treat Shipyard. The following newspapers had information regarding the shipwreck of the SUSANNAH, including the Passenger List. These are available in the microprint section at the Fogler Library, University of Maine, Orono:

The Oracle of the Day (Portsmouth, New Hampshire), Saturday, October 27, 1798, p. 3, Ship News,

New Hampshire Gazette, October 31, 1798, p.3, "Melancholly" section,

Columbian Centinel (Boston), Wednesday, October 31, 1798, p. 1,

Salem Gazette (Massachusetts), Friday, November 16, 1798.

Please note that the schooner SUSANNAH has also been referred to as the SUSANNA and the SUKEY (See Chapter Six). The SUSANNAH was probably named for the owner's wife,

Appendix 2

Susannah (Ellingwood) Hitchborn, who was born in Boston on April 8, 1744 and is buried in the "Old Graveyard on the Common" in Boston. From the *Salem Gazette,* November 16, 1798 are the following passengers:

1. **Master: Captain Daniel Jameson**, age 35, was the son of James and Eleanor Stuart (Campbell) Jameson. He was born July 20, 1763 in Freeport, Maine [48]. At the time of his death, he was living in Bangor (today Orono), Maine near the Jameson Falls (named for Captain Jameson) and had just built a new log cabin (on land currently owned by the University of Maine) for his wife and family. He was married to Elizabeth (Colburn) Jameson, daughter of Jeremiah and Frances (Hodgkins) Colburn. She was born in Pownalborough, April 26, 1762. They had four children:

   a. Jeremiah (1785-1861);
   b. Daniel, Jr., (d. in 1872);
   c. Fanny, (married William Colburn, Jr., November 2, 1816);
   d. Martin, (died in Richibucto, New Brunswick).

It was also reported the Captain Jameson kept a tavern in the first frame house in Bangor, built by Jedidiah Preble. This tavern was believed to have been the first Bangor tavern and was located just south of Cascade Park [48 and 12, p. 208]. Mentioned in the "Melancholly" section was an umbrella marked, "D. Jameson," which had washed up on shore. Famous Penobscot Tribal leader, Joseph Orono, died at the Robert Treat truck-house in Bangor on February 5, 1801. Brewer resident Fannie Hardy Eckstorm wrote in *Maine – A History* (Volume I), Chapter III, 1919:

> [Penobscot] Tribal traditions say that . . . [Joseph Orono's] place of burial is unknown, but tradition says that it was upon the farm of the old *[Daniel] Jameson* place in Stillwater.

2. **Robert Treat, Jr.,** age 19, was the son of Major Robert Treat (1753-1824) and Mary (Partridge) Treat (1758-1801). He was born in the Kenduskeag Plantation (later Bangor) on August 1, 1779, during the time of the tragic Penobscot Expedition of

Passenger List – Shipwreck SUSANNAH

1779. (For more information on the worst naval defeat in American history prior to Pearl Harbor, see *The Penobscot Expedition*, (2002) by George E. Buker [77].) His father was the first boat-builder in Bangor and built the schooner on which his oldest son lost his life. The SUSANNAH was built in Bangor at the Robert Treat boatyard in 1791 and was launched in 1793 when purchased by Robert Hichborn, Sr. This vessel was a two-masted topsail schooner and was five years old at the time of the shipwreck off the coast of Cape Ann. Reported on the "Melancholly" list were clothes marked "R.T." which had washed on shore [12, p. 1316].

3. **Francis Haynes** – I have been unable to obtain information regarding this passenger. The newspaper report stated that he was from the Bangor area. There is a Catherine Haynes who owned Lot #2 on the Park Holland Survey Map of 1801, and her deed states that she was a minor and her executor was a John Haynes. A Mrs. Haynes is listed in Robert Treat's truck house daybook [12, p. 1065]. This book had records of accounts from settlers up and down the Penobscot River and Bay, from 1773 to 1800.

4. **Seth Noble, Jr.**, age 21, was born August 5, 1777 in Sheffield (Sunbury County), Nova Scotia (today New Brunswick), Canada. He was the firstborn child of Seth and Hannah (Barker) Noble. Seth Noble and his family left Bangor in 1797, but Seth, Jr. decided to stay in Bangor in the home and on the land where his mother was buried. Rev. Seth Noble never sold the land on which this home was built. Seth, Jr. had been living in Bangor since he was nine years old, and Lucius Boltwood reported that "he was universally loved by all [2, p. 211]." It was reported that he was shipping lumber from Bangor to Boston at the time of the shipwreck. Bangor was just starting to realize the enormous wealth to be acquired from wood harvest and eventually became the lumber capital of the world in the early nineteenth century. The SUSANNAH was built within view of the Noble home, and it is quite possible that Seth, Jr., and his father participated in its construction. The *New Hampshire Gazette* (October 31, 1798, p. 3) reported that his "chests of clothes marked Mr. S. Noble, Jr.,"

washed up on shore and were later retrieved (at Halibut Point, Cape Ann) by his grieving father.

5. **Beriah Clapp**, age 29 (?), resided in Eddington (across the river from Bangor) and in Middleboro, Massachusetts. He was married to Nancy Pratt Wild Clapp and had three children, who were ages fourteen, eight, and five when their father went down on the SUSANNAH:

   a. Billings Clapp, (born October 24, 1790, died in Enfield, February 21, 1873);
   b. Nancy Clapp (born Walpole, Massachusetts, May 3, 1784, married Ware Eddy in 1809, died March 23, 1829);
   c. Beriah Clapp, Jr. (married Sylvia Eddy).

Beriah Clapp's estate was appraised on July 24, 1799. Besides his Estate in Eddington, he had a 14 acre lot in Middleboro, which was sold for $150. Widow Nancy Wild Clapp married Nathaniel McMahon on March 20, 1800 and had five more children. She died in Eddington, December 8, 1826, age 55 [12, p. 1059]. His chest of clothes also washed up on shore with the name, "Mr. B. Clapp."

6. **Joseph Potter**, age 28 (?), was the firstborn child of Joseph Potter and Margaret (Stinson) Potter of Topsam, Maine. Joseph Potter, Sr. was the direct descendant and fourth generation of Anthony Potter, who came to America seventeen years after the Pilgrims landed in Plymouth and settled in Ipswich, Massachusetts. They moved to Ellsworth, Maine in 1768, where Joseph Jr. is assumed to have been born. The Potter family relocated to Bangor after the Revolution. Joseph Potter's father, Joseph Potter, Sr., built the first sawmill in Bangor on the Kenduskeag Stream. Joseph Potter, Sr., died in 1788 and left an estate and sawmill to his wife. Joseph and Margaret (Stinson) Potter were married in Topsam in 1767 and had three sons: Joseph, William, and David (born in Kenduskeag Plantation, 1782) [12, Vol. VIII, p. 44]. Colonel Jonathan Eddy, Esq. (Justice of the Peace), married Joseph Potter, Jr., to Rhoda Mann, both of Bangor, on October 18, 1796. His death occurred on the exact date

of the second anniversary of his marriage to Rhoda. Rhoda (Mann) Potter left no record in Bangor after her husband's death.

7. **Richard Hall**, age 24, a resident of Medford, Massachusetts, son of Ebenezer Hall (1748-1831) and Martha (Jones) Hall [70]. He was born February 24, 1774 in Medford, and at the time of his death he was unmarried and listed as a merchant [70]. A hat and umbrella with "R. Hall" on it washed up on shore. His funeral sermon was preached by Rev. Dr. Osgood of Medford, from Job 14:19,

> *The waters wear the stone: thou washest away the things which grow out of the dust of the earth; and thou destroyest the hope of man [70, p. 21].*

Since a mention of a funeral service is made in the *Halls of New England, Genealogical and Biographical (1883) [70],* one of the five bodies that washed ashore may have been that of Richard Hall (See discussion of *The Oracle of the Day* report in Chapter Six, p. 70). No further mention of these five bodies has been found in any records of the Cape May area.

8. **Jonathan Brown,** from Cambridge, Massachusetts.

9. **Joshua Bangs**, age 23, was born in 1775, the firstborn child of Joshua Bangs and Mary (Hatch) Bangs [49]. His father died in Rhode Island in 1778 when he was only 3 years old. He had a sister, Sarah (Bangs) Snow [49]. He resided in Harwick, Massachusetts at the time of his death [49, p. 66]. A box marked "Joshua Bangs" washed up on shore.

10. **Oliver Deverix,** Boston, Massachusetts. Clothes marked "O. D." washed up on shore.

11. **Master John Pulling, Jr.,** was the youngest son of Sarah and John Pulling of Boston. John Pulling, Sr., was the famous warden of the Christ Church (North Church) who signaled by lantern to his friend Paul Revere. This is beautifully

Appendix 2

remembered in Henry Wadsworth Longfellow's poem written in 1861, "**Paul Revere's Ride**":

> ... *He said to his friend, "If the British march*
> *By land or sea from the town to-night,*
> *Hang a lantern aloft in the belfry arch*
> *Of the North Church tower as a signal light, –*
> *One if by land, and two if by sea;*
> *And I on the opposite shore will be,*
> *Ready to ride and spread the alarm*
> *Through every Middlesex village and farm,*
> *For the country folk to be up and to arm."* ...

12. **Miss Sarah Pulling,** age 25, was the oldest child of Sarah and John Pulling of Boston. She was born October 24, 1773, and one must conclude that she and her brother John, Jr. were visiting with the Hichborn family in Stockton Springs, Maine. Robert Hichborn and Paul Revere were first cousins and both were old friends of John and Sarah Pulling [41].

13. **Susannah (Susan) Hitchborn/Hichborn,** age 24, of Stockton Springs, was born in 1774 in Boston to Robert Hitchborn (1739-1800) and Susannah (Ellingwood) Hitchborn (1744-after 1800 and buried in Boston) [46]. Her father purchased Cape Jellison (Stockton Springs) in 1791 and built a large home there in 1792. It is believed that the SUSANNAH was his first schooner he had commissioned in the District of Maine and built by Robert Treat in Bangor in 1791 and launched in 1793. He named her SUSANNAH for Susan's mother, Susannah (Ellingwood) Hichborn. One of the most tragic aspects of this shipwreck is the Hichborn family oral history that Susan was on her way to be married in Boston. It is supposed that many passengers were part of her wedding party. It was also reported that clothes washed on shore were marked "S.H." and that her trunk also washed up on shore with "S.H." in brass-headed nails on the top and was retrieved by her betrothed who traveled to Cape Ann from Boston [46 and 50]. (Please contact this author if anyone knows the name of Susan Hichborn's fiancé!)

Passenger List – Shipwreck SUSANNAH

14. Elizabeth (Eliza) Hitchborn/Hichborn, age 13, was born in 1785 in Boston to Robert and Susannah (Ellingwood) Hichborn. Eliza was the younger sister of Susan and she was on the way to Boston to be part of her sister's wedding. Reported in the Ellis book on Stockton Springs [50, p. 101], is a packet named "SUSAN AND ELIZA" which was built by Robert Hichborn in Stockton Springs and supposedly launched in 1794, and then sunk with the two sisters and two nieces on board. It is obvious that these two packets have been confused. If there had been a packet named the "SUSAN AND ELIZA," I believe that it was not launched in 1794, but rather after 1798 to honor the two sisters who were lost at sea aboard the SUSANNAH in 1798.

15. Sarah (Susan?) Hitchborn/Hichborn, age 5, was most likely the child of Philip Hitchborn (older brother of Susan and Eliza) and Betsey (Hopkins) Hitchborn, born in 1793 in Stockton Springs (then Prospect), District of Maine. She was a young niece to Susan and Eliza, on her way to Aunt "Susie's" wedding.

16. Mrs. S. Stevenson, of Boston.

17. Sylvia Knapp, age 29, of Brewer (then Orrington) whose name was not mentioned on the passenger list, but is included here as her name is mentioned in the Noble, Treat, and Knapp family genealogies as being aboard the ill-fated vessel. She was born in Mansfield, Massachusetts on December 11, 1769 and was the firstborn child of Samuel Knapp (1747-1827) and Rachel (Grover) Knapp (1746-1837). At the time of her death they resided in a log cabin near the land where I had resided for twenty-five years in Brewer. After Sylvia died, the family relocated to the town of Bradley [12, Vol. VI, p. 94].

18. Unknown passenger thought to be from a small town outside of Boston.

19. Unknown passenger thought to be a seaman belonging to the vessel.

Appendix 2

20. **Unknown passenger** thought to be a seaman belonging to the vessel.

From the *New Hampshire Oracle of the Day,* Ship News section, Portsmouth, New Hampshire, Saturday, October 29, 1798:

> *We hear that Sat. Night, the Schooner Sukey [nickname for Susannah] of Boston was wrecked on Sandy Bay near Cape Ann and every soul on Board perished and that five of the bodies have since driven on shore.*

As one looks over the names of the passengers whose lives were lost on October 18, 1798 off the coast of Cape Ann, you cannot help but be struck by the magnitude of the loss to Bangor and the surrounding area. Death, at this time period, was no stranger, but the loss of this many young lives was so great that it is a puzzle to me why this has been completely lost in time. If it had not been for a notation in Rev. Mr. Noble's diary, this shipwreck might never have come to light. The SUSANNAH carried so many friends and relatives of Paul Revere that one's mind could leap to a British plot of revenge. What this shipwreck actually speaks to is the courage that our early pioneers in Maine not only demonstrated on land, but also on the sea. The enormous danger of sailing New England coastal waters without our current navigational systems is unimaginable. Just take a glance at a map of the coast of Maine and you will marvel that more ships were not lost.

This brings to mind the sermon Seth Noble wrote and delivered in 1774:

> *If a people will not hear His first judgments; . . .*
> *if they take no notice of these, He takes away the first born, . . . and sweeps them away to heaven [34].*

Seth Noble must have recalled this early sermon of "God's taking of the firstborn," and one can only imagine the torment that must have gone through his mind. The majority of the passengers were firstborns, and did he believe that they had been sacrificed for the "sins of the fathers?" Did he think that this was God's way of speaking to him?

Rev. Seth Noble returned to the Penobscot River and presided over a eulogy at the Hichborn home in Stockton Springs. It was also reported that he came back to Bangor, where Hannah was buried, and gave a service to honor the many young men and women who perished including his beloved Seth, Jr. What a sad departure from Bangor, Seth Noble was forced to repeat!

Appendix 3

Sheet Music, Maps, Photos, and Documents

Pertaining to the Life of Rev. Seth Noble

A Collection of the best Psalm Tunes by Josiah Flagg and engraved
by Paul Revere, 1764, Boston, Preface and BANGOR Tune [28]................119

The American Harmony or Royal Melody Complete by William Tans'ur,
1771, seventh edition, printed and sold by Daniel Bayley,
Newbury-Port, Massachusetts [29]...122

The Royal Melody Complete or the New Harmony of Zion, by.
William Tans'ur, third edition, Boston, printed and sold by
W. M. Alpine, including BANGOR Tune and list other Tans'ur
Tunes, courtesy of Newburyport Public Library, Newburyport,
Massachusetts..124

An Elegy on SOPHRONIA, who died with the Small-Pox, by
Dr. Isaac Watts (1674-1748) including P. M. SOPHRONIA Tune,
courtesy of Philip Mead (see pp. 48-50)...127

Birthplace and childhood home of Rev. Seth Noble, Westfield,
Massachusetts, from Lucius M. Boltwood [2], home is no longer
in existence..130

Cover page of Rev. Seth Noble 1774 sermon [34] in Rev. Seth
Noble's own handwriting, (see p. 5)..131

Private Seth Noble Muster Rolls, courtesy of J. J. Noble.........................132

Private Seth Noble Muster Rolls for Captain Jabez West
and his Machias militia, courtesy of J. J. Noble.....................................133

Rev'd Seth Noble Deposition in Boston, 1777 Battle of Machias
before Joseph Greenleaf, Justice of the Peace, Boston (see p.19)................134

Appendix 3

1784 Letter of support for land grant to the future town of
Eddington, signed by John Hancock and Samuel Adams [71].....................135

1787 **Sunbury** Petition to the General Court of Massachusetts,
name rejected by the court by 1788 [12, Vol. I, p. 11].............................136

1789 Condeskeag Plantation Petition asking for tax relief due to post-
Revolutionary War poverty and other hardships [12, Vol. VI, p. 171]...........137

1793 Engraving of the Old State House, rebuilt in 1712 and
is the site of the General Court of Massachusetts and birthplace
of Bangor in 1791...139

1790 **Bangor** Petition for Incorporation, written and delivered
by Seth Noble, agent for the Kenduskeag Plantation (May 18, 1790),
early photocopy courtesy of the Bangor Historical Society, and
[12, Vol. I, p. 12]..140

**1791 Bangor Incorporation Charter, February 25, 1791
(Birth Certificate of Bangor, Maine)**...144

Signers of the Bangor 1791 Incorporation Charter, (David Cobb,
Samuel Phillips, and Governor John Hancock)......................................146

Warrant for First Bangor Town Meeting, February 25, 1792
and Notice [12, Vol I, p. 13]...147

Colonel Jonathan Eddy, biographical sketch, memorial in Eddington,
engraving from the *History of Penobscot County* [51], and portrait from
the family of the late Robert Eddy, M. D. of Camden, Maine, photo by
C. B. Smith Fisher..148

One of five rejected petitions from Rev. Seth Noble to the General
Court for mandated land on which to build his church, courtesy of
Massachusetts Archives..151

1767 Map of Nova Scotia showing location of Sunbury County
and Maugerville, courtesy of Ann Flewelling..152

1795 Map of the District of Maine (Commonwealth of Massachusetts)
Maine did not receive statehood until 1820..153

1779 Map of Penobscot Bay at the time of the Penobscot
Expedition by Kenneth and Carol Fisher...154

1801 Park Holland Plan in the Office of the Register of Deeds,
Penobscot County, Maine [51] with settlers lots who settled in
Bangor prior to 1798, showing Seth Noble's original Lot 15....................155

Appendix 3

1801 Survey of Refugee Land in Franklinton (Columbus), Ohio, (see Seth Noble lots 13, and 32), courtesy of Franklin County Historical Society..156

1803 Franklin County, Ohio, Map by Suzanne Mettle, courtesy of Franklin County Historical Society................................... 157

Early Ohio Land Deeds (1802) to Seth Noble from Thomas Jefferson and James Madison, courtesy of J. J. Noble.....................158

"Noble Ladies" return to Bangor, descendants of Rev. Seth and Hannah Noble (Joanne Schotthoefer, Murphy Schotthoefer Florence Irene Sihksnel) and Rev. Seth Noble (a.k.a. Ken Fisher), for presentation ceremony of newly discovered 1791 Bangor Charter, Sept. 22, 2003, Bangor City Hall, photo by C. B. Smith Fisher......................160

City of Bangor, Maine **Proclamation** recognizing Carol B. Smith Fisher for discovering and returning Bangor's 1791 original Charter for Incorporation, from the Massachusetts Archives, Boston..........................161

Rev. Seth Noble (Kenneth P. Fisher), Sept. 22, 2003, photo taken in Brewer, Maine in front of the exact location of Rev. Seth Noble's church, built in 1794, only stones are left to mark the site, photo by C. B. Smith Fisher..162

Photo of Hannah Noble (Gorham) Beach, born in Kenduskeag Plantation (Bangor) Sept. 11, 1789 to Hannah and Seth Noble, died Nov. 17, 1854, age 65, in Amity, Ohio, photo courtesy of J. J. Noble, via Hannah descendant, R.W. Parrott...............................163

1901 photo of Harry Gordon Noble, great grandson of Hannah and Seth Noble, photo courtesy of J. J. Noble..164

Photo of Canadian Ambassador John Joseph Noble, great, great great grandson of Hannah and Seth Noble. 165

1996 photo of United Church of Canada, formerly the Congregational Church of Maugerville and then moved to Sheffield, Sunbury County, New Brunswick, Canada. Church of first minister, Rev. Seth Noble, photo courtesy of George H. Hayward, ...166

Log cabin similar to what Seth Noble might have first built in the Kenduskeag Plantation in 1786, photo by Wayne Killam at the Maine Forest & Logging Museum, Inc., Leonard's Mills, Bradley, Maine..168

Appendix 3

1771 home of Col. John Brewer (609. South Main Street, Brewer, Maine). Seth Noble and wife Hannah Barker Noble first stayed in this home before moving to their log cabin in Bangor in 1786, photo by C.B. Smith Fisher..169

Headstone of Col. John Brewer in Oak Hill Cemetery in Brewer, Maine. The founding father of Brewer was a close friend of Seth Noble, and partly responsible for Seth Noble's arrival in the Penobscot River communities, photo by C. B. Smith Fisher.......................170

Model of topsail two-masted schooner resembling the SUSANNAH, (The EAGLE, by Gary Beckwith, from Cape Elizabeth), photo by C. B. Smith Fisher, ...…..171

Robert Hichborn, Sr. headstone in the Cape Jellison Cemetery, Stockton Springs, Maine (owner of the schooner SUSANNAH and became the first burial in his donated cemetery land), photo C. B. Smith Fisher.....................…..172

Seth Noble's Bangor and Penobscot River 218 years later! Photo courtesy of the Bangor Area Chamber of Commerce by E. Michael Youngblood Photography...173

Seth Noble's Franklinton (Columbus), Ohio, overlooking the Scioto River 202 years later! Photo courtesy of Rod Berry Photography and Experience Columbus...174

NOBLE STREET, site of land and log cabin of Rev. Seth Noble, the brick building is the Columbus Arts Center today and the former Ohio State Arsenal built in 1861. Photo by Rod Berry Photography, provided by courtesy of Experience Columbus...175

Appendix 3

A Collection of the Best Psalm Tunes by Josiah Flagg
and engraved by Paul Revere, 1764

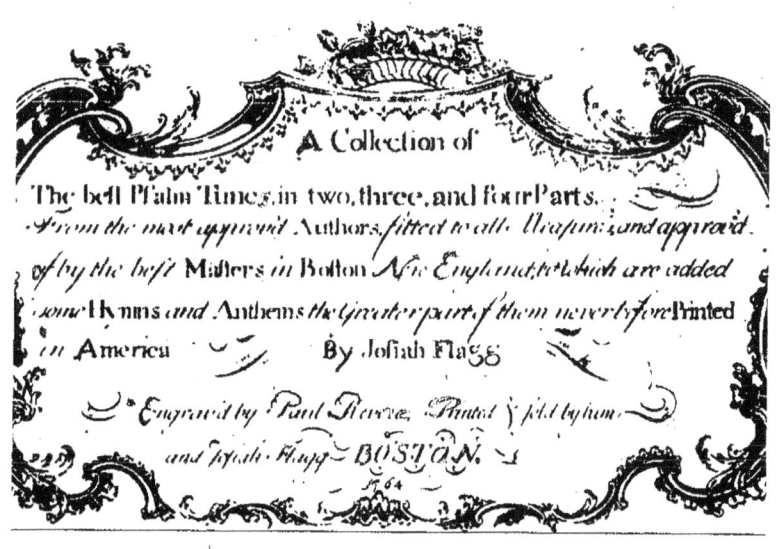

Appendix 3

Preface to Best Psalm Tunes, 1764

PREFACE

... ought necessary, that some Apology should be made, for offering to ... Collection of Psalm Tunes, at a Time when there are already so many among us: The Editor has only this to say in general, that he has endeavoured, according to the best of his Judgment, to extract the Sweets out of a Variety of fragrant Flowers: He has taken from every Author be has seen, a few Tunes, which be judges to be the best, and compriz'd them within the Compass of a small Pocket Volume; bow far be bas succeeded in this Attempt, he leaves to the candid Masters of Musick to determine: If ... is so fortunate as to meet with their Approbation, with Regard to the Choice be ... made, he begs Leave, upon the Suppossition, just to make this Remark, That as the Tun... were compos'd by different masterly Hands, the Air of them is various, which afford... Reason to Hope they will not fail of gratifying ... some Measure Persons of every Taste.

TO comply with the Request of some, the Tenor Part is ... the G Cliff: The Rules laid down, tho' concise, are plain, and contain the whole th... ary.

IT is hoped, it will not diminish the Value of this Book ... Estimation of any, but may in some Degree recommend it even to those who ... peculiar Relish for Musick, That however we are oblig'd to ... Side th... ick chiefly, for our Tunes, the Paper on which they are ... is the Manu... our own Country.

Appendix 3

BANGOR Tune by William Tans'ur from Best Psalm Tunes

Appendix 3

The American Harmony or Royal Melody Complete
by Wm. Tans'ur [29], Original Title Page, 1771

THE
American Harmony:
OR
Royal Melody Complete.

IN TWO VOLUMES.

VOL. I. CONTAINING;

I. A *New* and *Correct* INTRODUCTION to the *Grounds* of MUSICK; *Rudemental, Practical* and *Technical*.
II. A *New* and *Complete* Body of CHURCH MUSICK, adapted to the most select *Portions* of the BOOK of PSALMS, of either *Versions*; with many *Fuging Chorus's*, and *GloriaPatri's* to the whole.
III. A *New* and *Select Number* of HYMNS, ANTHEMS, and CANONS; suited to several Occasions; and many of them never before printed; Set by the greatest *Masters* in the World.

The Whole are composed in *Two, Three, Four,* and *Five* Musical Parts, according to the nicest *Rules*; consisting of *Solo's, Fuges* and *Chorus's*, correctly set in *Score* for *Voices* or *Organ*; and fitted for all *Teachers, Learners,* and Musical SOCIETIES, &c.

The SEVENTH EDITION, with Additions.

By WILLIAM TANS'UR, Senior, *Musico Theorico*.

Psal. cxlix { O Praise ye the LORD, *prepare your glad Voice* ; *His* Praise *in the* Great Assembly *to sing,* } Ver. I.
in our Great CREATOR, *let Is'r'el rejoice* ; *And Children of* ZION *be glad in their* KING.

Printed and Sold by DANIEL BAYLEY, at his House next Door to St. Paul's Church, Newbury-Port. Sold also by most Booksellers in *Boston*.

Appendix 3

Bangor Tune, American Harmony, 1771

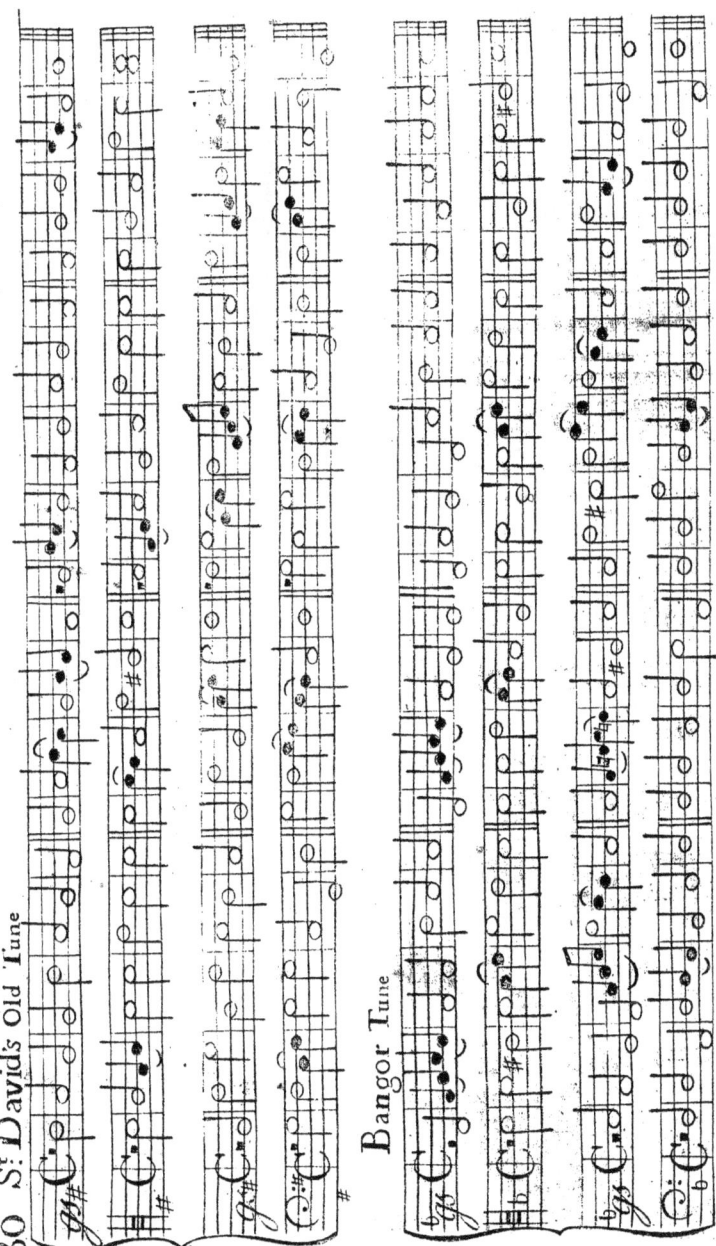

Appendix 3

The Royal Melody Complete: New Harmony of Zion, 1767
By William Tans'ur

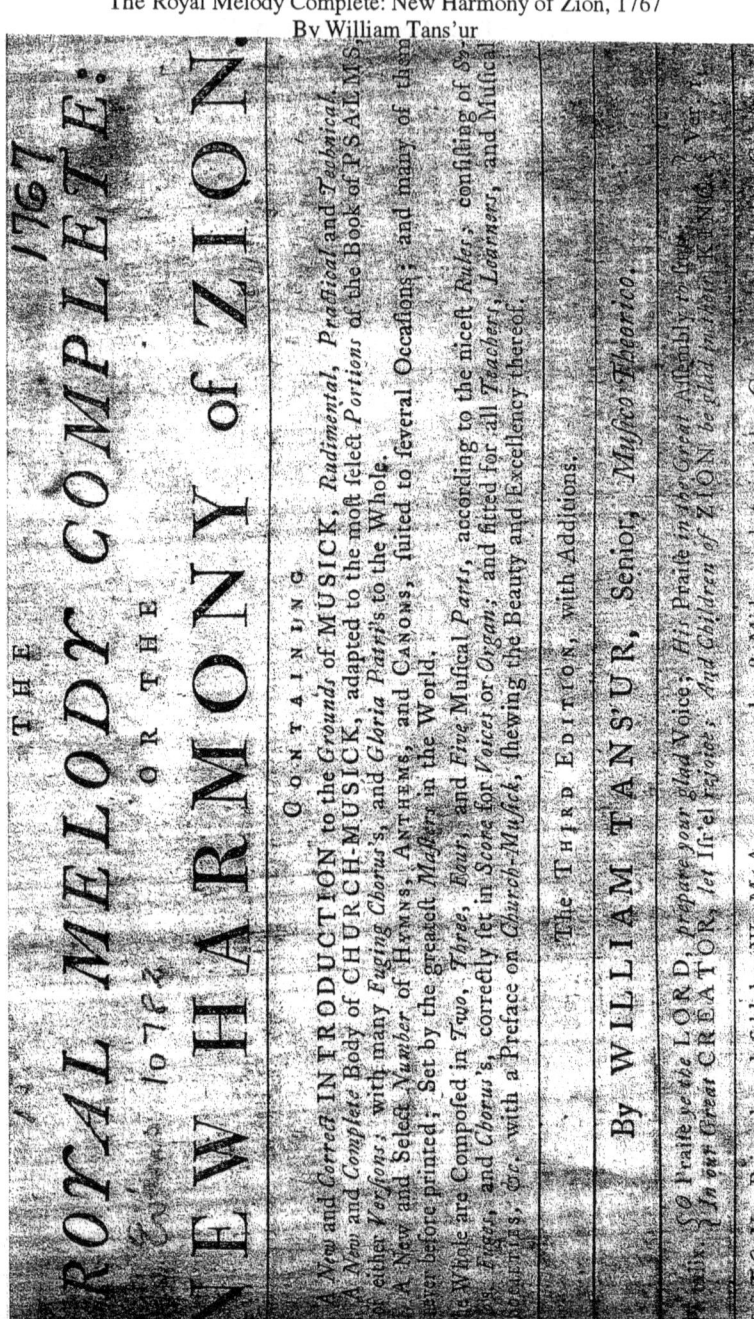

Appendix 3
BANGOR Tune, 1767

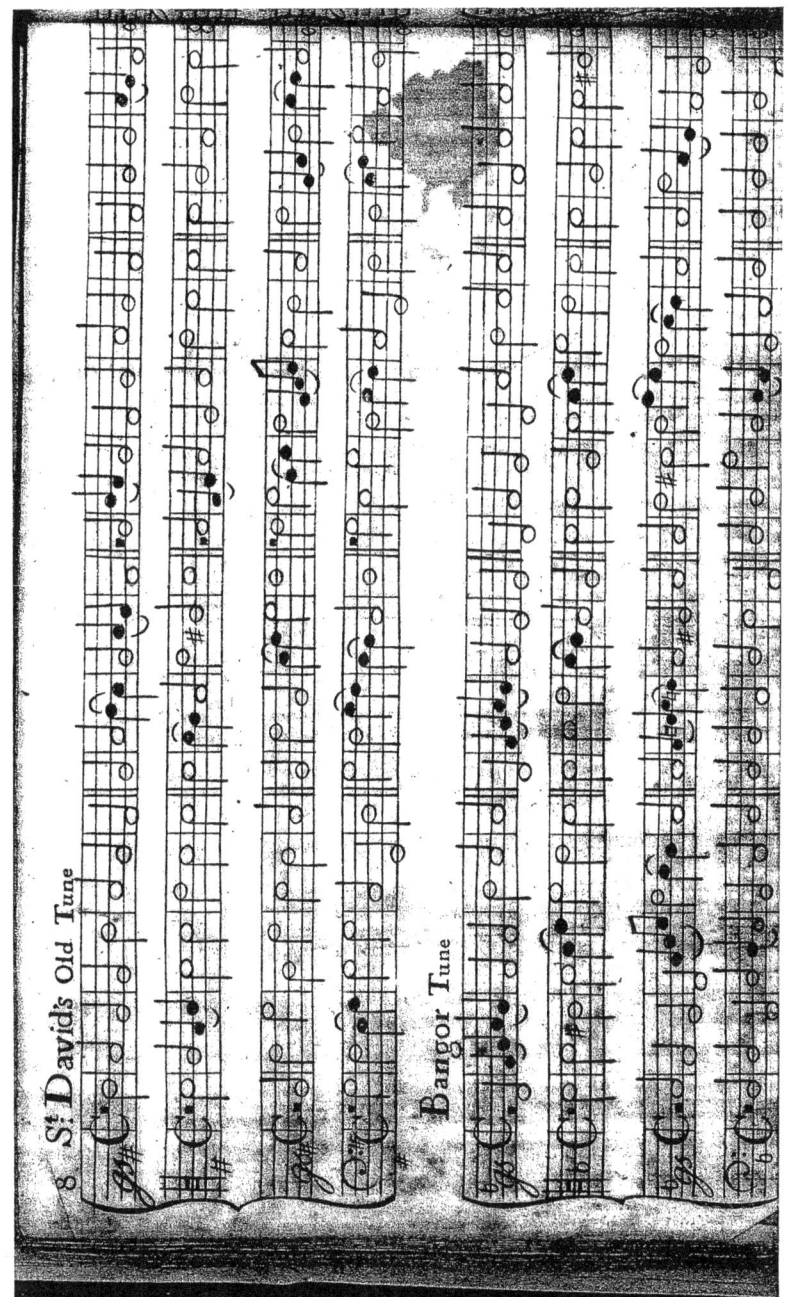

Appendix 3
List of other William Tans'ur Hymn Tunes, 1767

Tune	Page
ALL Saints Tune	12
St. Aleph Tune	31
Axminster Tune	28
Angles Hymn, Thought of	
Belford Tune	7
Bangor Tune	37
Bridengrove Tune	30
Leominster Tune	6
Baxby Tune	15
Bedford Tune	39
Bicchester Tune	11
Blenheim Tune	22
Babylon Tune	40
Christ-Church Tune	28
Chellerton Tune	26
Dunchurch Tune	19
S. David's Tune	56
Dorchester Tune	30
Durham Tune	13
St. David's (New)	24
S. Edmund's Tune	31
Ewell Tune	16
Exeter Tune	10
Evening Hymn	23
Falmouth Tune	8
Few Happy Matches	10
Goddard Tune	8
Hereford Tune	18
Hertford Tune	9
Kirkelton Tune	14
St. Katherine's Tune	9

Tune	Page
Kingston Tune	40
Landaff Tune	34
Lemster Tune	12
St. Luke's Tune	27
St. Martin's Tune	14
Manchester Tune	85
St. M'chael's Tune	32
Marlborough Tune	25
Mansfield Tune	92
Morning Hymn or Evening	7
Newbury Tune	6
St. Neot's Tune	5
Oakham Tune	17
Ragby Tune	24
Rutland Tune	22
Rothwell a *Morning Hymn*	33
Ryball Tune	29
Sion Tune	5
Savoy Tune	33
Totrington Tune	16
Tamworth Tune	30
Trinity Tune	35
Upminster Tune	21
Uppingham Tune	2
Winchester Tune	36
Wortlop Tune	37
Windsor Tune	11
Westerham Tune	20
Wendover Tune	38
Yaxley Tune	ib
Zealand Tune	35

Tune	Page
Banbury	
Bray	93 Killingworth 85
Bedford	95 Latterworth 96
Chelmsford	89 New-port 88
Darlington	84 Pordmouth 89
Ely	88 Quinzay 92
Farnham	93 Ulcexter 93
Ixworth	96 Wantage 95
	84 Wellingborō 85
	Woodflock 81

ANTHEMS

Blessed are they that are pure	68
Behold I bring ye Tidings	62
God be merciful unto us	70
Give the King thy Judgments	49
I will love Thee, O Lord, my	41
I was glad when they said	54
I will magnify Thee	82
O give ye Thanks unto the Lord	80
O Clap your Hands together	60
O Praise the Lord of Heaven	57
O Praise the Lord, O my Soul	74
Praise the Lord, O my Soul	94
Rejoice in the Lord	65
Sing ye merrily unto God	45
They that go down to the Sea	78
When *Israel* came out of *Egypt*	90

Appendix 3

An Elegy on **SOPHRONIA**, who died with the Small-Pox
By Dr. Isaac Watts (1674-1748)
1711

FORBEAR, my friends, forbear, and ask no more,
    Where all my cheerful airs are fled:

Why will ye make me talk my torments o'er?
    My joy, my life, my comfort's dead.

Deep from my soul, mark how the sobs arise,
    Hear the long groans that waste my breath,

And read the mighty sorrow in my eyes,
    Lovely Sophronia sleeps in death.

Unkind disease, to vail that rosy face
    With tumours of a mortal pale;

While mortal purples, with their dismal grace,
    And double horrors spot the vail.

Uncomely vail, and most unkind disease?
    Is this Sophronia, once the fair?

Are these the features that were born to please?
    And beauty spread her ensigns there?

I was all love and she was all delight,
    Let me run back to season past;

Ah! flowery days, when first she charmed my fight!
    But roses will not always last.

Yet still Sophronia pleased. Nor time nor care
    Could take her youthful bloom away:

Virtue has charms which nothing can impair;
    Beauty like her's could ne'er decay.

Roots in a soil refin'd, grows high on earth,
    And blooms with life, and joy, and love.

Such was Sophronia's soul. Celestial dew.
    And angels' food, were her repast:

Devotion was her work, and thence she drew
    Delights which strangers never taste.

Not the gay splendors of a flattering court
    Could tempt her to appear and shine:

Her solemn airs forbid the world's resort:
    But I was blest, and she was mine.

Safe on her welfare all my pleasure hung,
    Her smiles could all my pains control;

Her soul was made of softness, and her tongue
    Was soft and gentle as her soul.

She was my guide, my friend, my earthly all;
    Love grew with every waning moon;

Had Heav'n a length of years delay'd its call,
    Still I had thought it call'd too soon.

But peace, my sorrows, not with murmuring voice
    Dare to accuse heav'ns high decree:

She was first ripe for everlasting joys;
    Sophron, she waits above for thee.

Appendix 3
SOPHRONIA Hymn Tune by Isaac Watts, 1711
(sung by Seth Noble for Hannah's eulogy in June 1790)

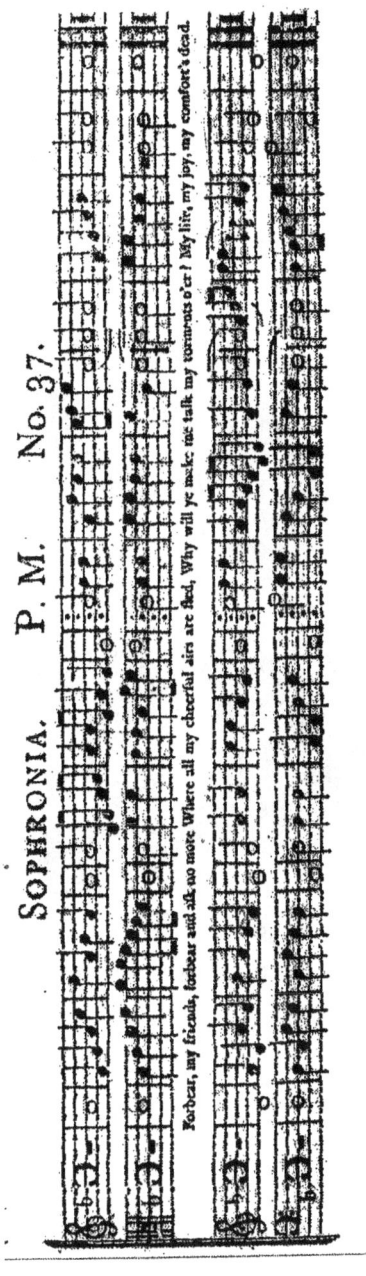

Appendix 3

Birthplace of Rev. Seth Noble, Westfield, Massachusetts

HOUSE OF THOMAS NOBLE, 3D, WESTFIELD, MASS.
BUILT ABOUT 1725.

Appendix 3
Cover Page, Rev. Seth Noble 1774 Sermon [34]

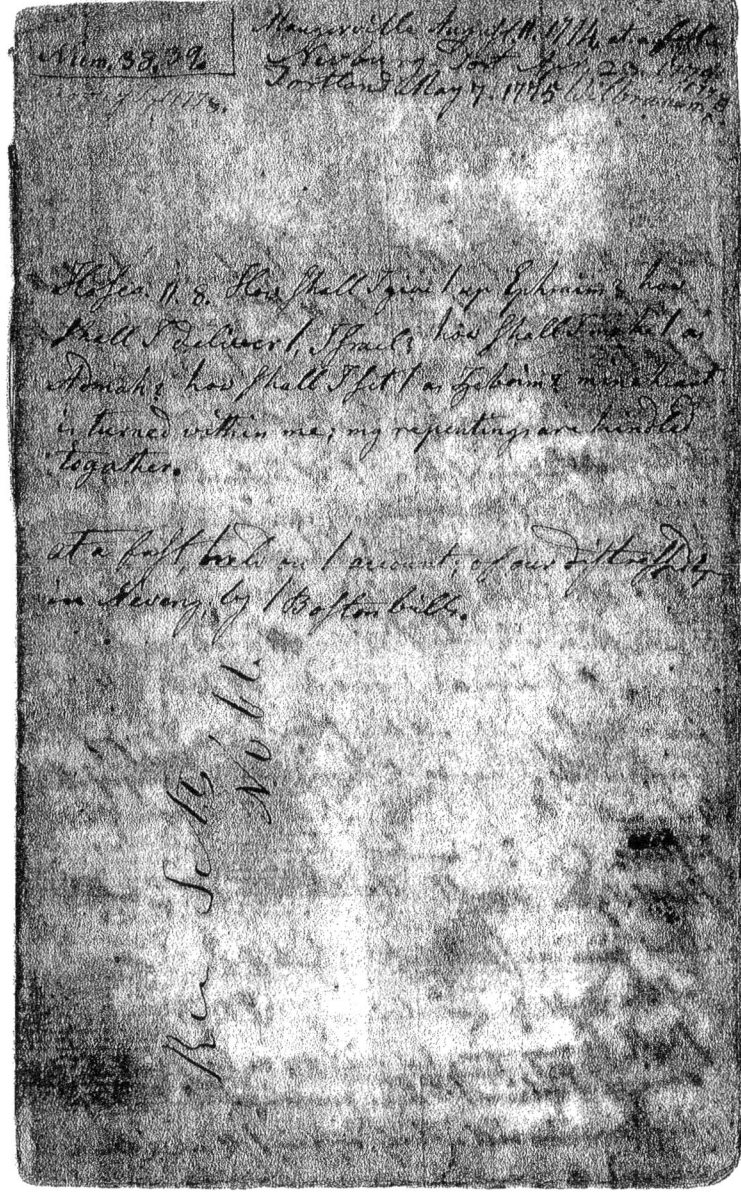

132 Appendix 3

Private Seth Noble Muster and Pay Rolls, 1777, Mass. Militia

Appendix 3

Private Seth Noble Muster Roll for Captain Jabez West Company raised in Machias, Aug. 5, 1777

Appendix 3

Deposition of Rev'd Seth Noble, 1777 Battle of Machias, (see p. 19)

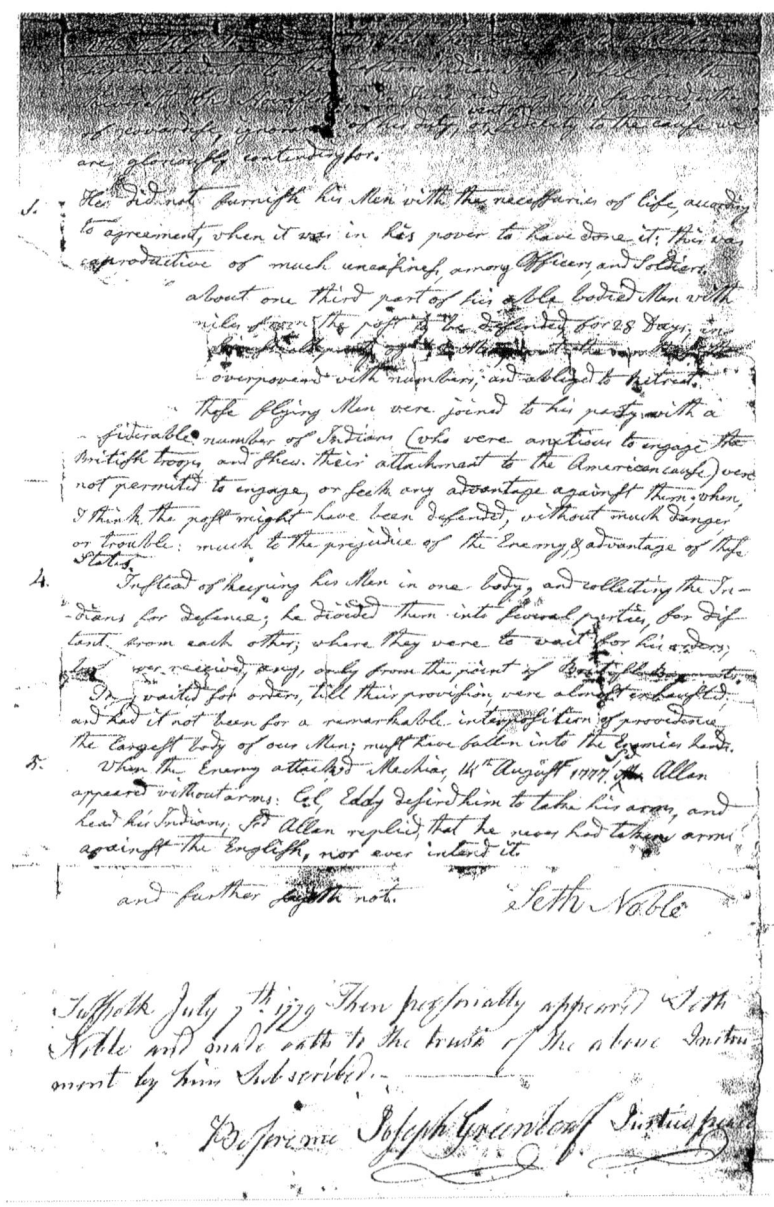

Appendix 3

Land Grant for future town of Eddington, Letter of Approval, 1784
From John Hancock and Samuel Adams (pp. 25-26)

Boston Feby 26. 1784   416

Gentn.

Col. Jonathan Eddy has informed us of his intention to petition Congress for the relief of certain Sufferers from Nova Scotia. We were at Congress at the time when these unhappy people were driven from that Province, & we have every reason to suppose that their misfortunes arose from an active zeal in the cause of America. Several of them have since served in the army & as we are informed have acquitted themselves with fidelity. It certainly would not be shewing a more just adherence to our unfortunate friends than has been shewn by the British to theirs, if the Petitioners should receive a reasonable compensation for their losses. We wish you to give them all the assistance in your power, & if any thing could be effected for them this spring it would afford them a relief which their immediate exigencies require.

We are with Sentiments of Esteem, Gentlemen, Your most Hum. Servts

John Hancock
Sam Adams

Hon. The Delegates in Congress from Massachusetts

Appendix 3

1787 Sunbury Petition to the General Court of the Commonwealth of Massachusetts

To the Honourable, the Senate; and House of Representatives in the Common-Wealth of the Massachusetts, in General-Court convened.

The petion [sic] of the subscribers: inhabitants off [sic]; and living upon a tract of Land in the County of Lincoln, - by the name number-two, in the second Range of Townships: lying on the Western side of Penobscot River: bounded as follows: viz. Southerly on Number One, Easterly on Penobscot-River, and Northerly on Governments Lands, as will appear by Cpt. Stones Survey.

Your petioners [sic] beg leave to inform, that honourable Legislative Body; that there is living upon S'd Lands about forty Families: who labour under many difficulties for want of being incorporated with town privileges; therefore humbly pray, your honours would consider our difficulties; and incorporate us into a Town: by the name of **Sunbury.**

Your petioners [sic] as in duty bound shall ever pray.

his	Abner Tibbets,
Ashbell X Harthorn,	Daniel Campbell
mark	James Budge
Levi Bradley	Daniel Spenser,
John Jones	Isaac Freese,
Jacob Bussell,	Abraham Freese,
Robert Treat	Silas Harthorn
John Smart	Archibald McPhetres,
Jacob Dennett	Archibald McPhetres, Jr.
Thos. Howard	Abraham Allen.
George Tibbets,	

Sunbury, *Sept. 11th, 1787.*
Andrew Webster, Clerk,

Endorsement on back of Petition:

To the care of Dr. Cony, Hallowell.
Sir, please to forward this Petion [sic] to the great and general Court, and you will oblige your Friends, the Petitioners [12, Vol. I, p.11].

[This petition to incorporate under the name of **Sunbury** was rejected prior to Oct. 6, 1788 as the town records show by Oct. 6, 1788 they called themselves Penobscot River, west side.]

Appendix 3

The following petition was found in the Bangor Historical Magazine - Vol. VI - Jan., Feb., March, 1891. It was found in the Massachusetts Archives by Dr. J. F. Pratt.

PETITION FROM CONDESKEAG PLANTATION

Condeskeag Plantation Dec. 31, 1789.

Hancock [Bangor was then part of Hancock County].

To the honorable the Senate house of Representatives of the Commonwealth of Massachusetts, in General Court convened:

The petition of Jethro Delano, (appointed as agent) for the freeholders of said Plantation of Condeskeag Humbly Sheweth; that whereas several tax bills hath lately been sent us requesting the speedy payment of considerable sums of money, for the exeginces of government, therefore your petitioner flatters himself, that a little attention to the following facts, will convince your honors that the request was premature.

*As legal subjects we **feel** for the exeginces of government; and could wish, it was in our power to cast in our mite for its relief.*

Believe we may truly affirm that no part of the United States of America, are so needy as we, our lands abound with large hemlock trees: which makes it difficult for poor people to clear, without the help of oxen. Where fish and lumber are plenty, people always are kept poor; because the purchaser reaps all the profit of the poor man's labor. No people ever venter'd to settle an inhospitable wilderness, in more needy circumstances, than this people without money, provisions or farming utensils. Necessity drove us to lumbering, and fishing for a support, which hath much retarded the cultivation of our lands.

In the late war, we had no succour; only from the British at Majabigwaduce at such enormous prices as considerably involved us in debt. Since the peace took place so many of our cattle have been taken to answer those demands at moderate prices, as renders the cultivation of our lands extremely difficult.

Many of us have no other way to break up our lands or get our grain into the ground but with the hoe. We're obliged (for several years) to labor considerable part of our time on the British garrison, both in seed time and harvest.

Had our cattle, sheep and swine, and wreck of household furniture frequently taken from us both by British and Americans, without any satisfaction; but such abusive language as if Heaven had deprived them. Those who tarried here and traded with the Britoners; were called rebels, the others who left their places, and went to the Westward, were called fools for leaving their property.

*Poverty at present deprives us from setting (a price) for what we have for market some think it oppresive, to be taxed for lands which we have no title to; nor the lest encouragement that we ever **shall** have, what encouragement have we, to make improvements on such lands, and what is a man's life worth, without the comforts and enjoyments of it. Being deprived of town priveleges, we are deprived of good orders consequently of roads for recreation, comfort or even necessity.*

Appendix 3

Not five bushels of bread corn to a family, through the whole settlements for the approaching winter. Could your honors come into our huts, fare as we do, and look upon our half naked children, we should need no other petition to have these taxes postponed; in fact it is morally impossible to raise the money now called for.

*These, gentlemen, are facts, wherefore your petitioner humbly prays that your honors would take our **needy** and difficult circumstances, into your wise considerations, and free us from State taxes for the present. Or otherwise order the same to be appropriated to the use of sd. plantation, (viz:) for the support of the gospel, schools, roads &c. And your petitioner as in duty bound, shall ever pray.*

[signed] *Jethro Delano,*
Agent for Sd. Plantation
[12, Vol. VI, p. 171]

Appendix 3

Appendix 3
1790 Seth Noble Bangor Petition for Incorporation

Penobscot-River 28. May. 1790.

To the honorable the Senate, and House of Representatives of the Common-Wealth of the Massachusetts in General Court assembled.

The petition of the subscribers, inhabitants of, and living upon a tract of Land in the County of Lincoln, by the name of number one second range lying on the West side of Penobscot-River: bounded as follows, viz.

Southerly on Number One, Easterly on Penobscot-River, Northerly, and Westerly on Governments Land, as will appear by Cpt. Stones survey —— Humbly sheweth, that there is living upon s.d Land forty-five Families, seventy-nine Polls; and possess of about two thirds of the Property, of what is commonly called Kenduskeag-Plantation; or the plantation from the Widdow-Wheelers-Mills and upward, to the head of the settlement, on the West side of Penobscot-River. We labour under many disadvantages for want of being incorporated with Town-privileges; therefore humbly pray, your Honours would be pleased to take our difficult circumstances, into your wise consideration; and incorporate us into a Town, by the name of Bangor. We have no justice of the Peace for thirty miles on this side of the shire, no Grand-Jurors, and some people not of the best, your Honours know what the consequences must be. We doubt not but you will grant us our request; and your Petioners as in duty bound shall ever pray.

Andrew Webster Clerk

P.S. The inhabitants of s.d Plantation at sundry legal meetings for two years past have unanimously voted to be incorporated; without which we can have no benefit, of our schools, or ministerial Lands.

In the House of Representatives June 8. 1790
Read & committed to the standing Committee on Incorporations of Towns &c. to consider & report
Sent up for concurrence

David Cobb Spkr

In Senate June 9. 1790
Read & concurred
S. Phillips Jr. Presid.

In the House of Representatives Jany 31. 1791
Read and committed to the standing
Committee on applications for ~~states~~ incorporations of Towns &c.
Sent up for concurrence
David Cobb Spr

In Senate Feby. 1. 1791
Read & Concurred
Saml Phillips Presidt

The petition of
S. M. Noble, Agent
for Kenduskeag plan-
tation. 1790 —
23
leave to bring in a bill

Com on Incorporations
of Towns.

Appendix 3

1790 BANGOR PETITION

To the Commonwealth of Massachusetts, written in the handwriting of Rev. Seth Noble and delivered by Rev. Mr. Noble, as Agent for the Kenduskeag Plantation to the General Court on June 7th, 1790.

Penobs - River 18. May, 1790.

To the honorable the Senate, and House of Representatives of the Common-Wealth of the Massachusetts in General Court assembled.

The petion [sic] of the subscribers, inhabitants off; and living upon a tract of Land in the County of Lincoln, by the name of number One, second rang lying on the West-Side of Penobscot-River: bounded as follows, viz.

Southerly on Number <u>One</u>, Easterly on Penobscot-River, <u>Northerly</u>, and <u>Westerly</u> on Government Land, as will appear by Cpt.-Stone's - survey. Humbly sheweth, that their is living upon s'd Land forty-five Families, Seventy nine-[?]; and are possessed of about two-thirds of the Property, of what is commonly called Kenduskeeg-Plantation; <u>or</u>, the plantation from the Widdow - Wheelers-Mills, and upward, to the head of the settlement, on the West-side of Penobscot-River. We labour under many disadvantages for want of being incorporated with Town-privileges; therefore humbly pray, your Honours would be pleased to take our difficult circumstances, into your wise consideration; and incorporate us into a Town, by the name of **Bangor.** *We have no justice of the Peace for thirty miles on this side of the river, no Grand-Jurymen, and some people not of the best morals. Your Honours know what the consequences must be. We doubt not but you will grant us our request; and your petioners [sic] as in duty-bound shall ever pray.*

Andrew Webster } Clerk

P.S. *The inhabitants of s'd plantation at sundry legal-meetings for two Years past have unanimously voted to be incorporated; without which we can have no benefit, of our school, or ministerial Lands.*

The petion [sic] of Seth Noble, Agent for Kenduskeag-plantation. 1790.

leave to bring in a Bill

Com. on Incorporations
Of Towns

Appendix 3   143

[upon receipt]

In the House of Representatives June 8, 1790
Read and committed to the standing Committee on
Incorporations of Towns ve. to consider & report
Sent up for concurrence
David Cobb Spk'r

In Senate June 9, 1790
Read & concurred
S. Phillips, Presid't.

In the House of Representatives Janry 31st, 1791
Read and committed to the standing Committee on
applications for incorporations of Towns ve.
Sent up for concurrence David Cobb Spk'r.

In Senate February 1st, 1791
Read and Concurred   Sam'l. Phillips, Presid't.

Committee on Incorporations of Towns -----------------

[This petition was found in the Massachusetts Archives in 1885 by Joseph W. Porter who copied it for his article in the Bangor Historical Magazine on the Municipal History of Bangor [12, Vol. I, p. 12]. In this article Mr. Porter reported that this document was written in the handwriting of Andrew Webster. In Mr. Porter's defense it would have been understandable to conclude that Andrew Webster drew up the document, as he is the only person to have signed it. Having just received four different documents in the handwriting of Rev. Seth Noble and being recently given a Bangor Historical Society 1952 copy of this petition from the Massachusetts Archives, I must now conclude that this document was clearly written by Rev. Seth Noble and signed by Andrew Webster, clerk, prior to leaving for Boston. It also appears that the name **Bangor** was left blank and written in at a later time, by Rev. Seth Noble. It now looks very clear that the name **Bangor** was chosen by Rev. Seth Noble. He possibly decided that a successful incorporation name would be granted if he had it verbally verified in Boston, prior to writing in his chosen name of **Bangor**.]

Appendix 3

Commonwealth of Massachusetts.

In the year of our LORD one thousand seven hundred & ninety one.

An Act to incorporate the plantation of Kenduskeag into a town by the name of Bangor.—

Be it enacted by the Senate and House of Representatives in General Court assembled and by the authority of the same, that the following described tract of land, viz— Beginning at a stake and stones on the bank of Penobscot river on the westerly side thereof, near Simon Crosby's, and at the corner of township number one in the first range, thence running northwest about two hundred rods to a small birch tree, then west on the north line of number one first range two miles and an half to a poplar tree, then north by number two in the second range six miles to a poplar tree, thence east six miles to a large white pine tree standing in a great bog, thence south thirty three degrees east three miles and an half to a small poplar on the bank of Penobscot river, then down the said river to the first mentioned bounds, together with the inhabitants thereon being they are hereby incorporated into a town by the name of Bangor, and the said town is hereby invested with all the powers, privileges and immunities which other towns in this Commonwealth do or may enjoy by law.

And be it further enacted by the authority aforesaid, that Jonathan Eddy Esq'. be and he is hereby empowered and required to issue his warrant directed to some suitable inhabitant of the said Bangor, to meet at some convenient time & place to chuse all such Officers as towns are by law required to chuse in the month of March or April annually.—

In the House of Representatives February 24, 1791

This Bill having had three several Readings passed to be Enacted.
David Cobb Spk'.

In Senate February 25, 1791—
This Bill having had two several readings, passed to be Enacted
Sam'. Phillips Presid'.

Approv'd,
John Hancock

COMMONWEALTH OF MASSACHUSETTS.

In the year *of our* LORD *one thousand seven hundred & ninety one.*

An Act *to incorporate the plantation of Kenduskeeg into a town by the name of* **Bangor.** —

Be it Enacted *by the Senate and House of Representatives in General Court assembled, and by the authority of the same, that the following described tract of land, viz. – Beginning at a stake and stones on the bank of Penobscot river on the westerly side thereof, near Simon Crosby's, and at the corner of township number one in the first range, thence running northwest about two hundred rods to a small birch tree, then west on the north line of number one first range two miles and an half to a poplar tree, then north by number two in the second range six miles to a poplar tree, thence east six miles to a large white pine tree standing in a great bog, thence south thirty three degrees east three miles and an half to a small poplar on the bank of Penobscot river, then down the said river to the first mentioned bounds, together with the inhabitants thereon be and they are hereby incorporated into a town by the name of* **Bangor,** *and the said town is hereby invested with all the powers, privileges and immunities which other towns in this Commonwealth do or may enjoy by law.* —

And be it further **enacted** *by the authority aforesaid, that Jonathan Eddy Esq. be and he is hereby empowered and required to issue his warrant directed to some suitable inhabitant of the said* **Bangor,** *to meet at some convenient time & place to chuse all such Officers as towns are by law required to chuse in the month of March or April annually.* —

In the House of Representatives February 24th 1791

This Bill having had three several Readings passed to be **Enacted**
 [Signed] *David Cobb Spk'r*

In Senate **February 25th 1791** –
This Bill having had two several readings, passed to be **Enacted.**
 [Signed] *Sam'l Phillips Presid't*

Approv'd,
 [Signed] *J O H N   H A N C O C K*
[Governor of the Commonwealth of Massachusetts]

Appendix 3

Signers of the 1791 Bangor Incorporation Charter
David Cobb, Speaker of the House of Representatives
Samuel Phillips, President, In Senate
John Hancock, Governor, Commonwealth of Massachusetts

Judge Samuel Phillips, Jr., 1752-1802

Portrait of John Hancock, One of the Founding Fathers, painted by the historical painter, John Singleton Copley

WARRANT FOR FIRST BANGOR TOWN MEETING - FEBRUARY 25, 1792

*Hancock ss. To Capt. James Budge of Bangor, in said County, Gentleman - - Greeting: Whereas, an act passed the General Court, in the State of Massachusetts, February the 25th Day, in the year of our Lord one thousand seven hundred and ninety-one, incorporated into a town a certain tract of Land known by the name of Condiskeag plantation, together with the inhabitants therein, by the name of **Bangor**; and called on me to issue a warrant to some suitable inhabitant of **Bangor**, to warn a meeting of the inhabitants at some convenient time and place, to choose such officers as towns are by law required to choose in the months of March and April annually. Therefore, in the Name of the Commonwealth you are Required to warn the above said inhabitants to meet at some convenient time and Place for the aforesaid purposes, and this shall be your sufficient Warrant for so Doing. Given under my hand and seal this 25th Day of February, in the year 1792.*

[Signed] *Jona. Eddy, Justice of the Peace.*

NOTICE OF FIRST TOWN MEETING IN BANGOR

Bangor, March the 12th, 1792.

In obedience to the within warrant to me Directed, I have warned the within named Inhabitants to meet at the Dwelling house of Major Robert Treat, on Thursday, the 22d day of March.

James Budge.

Appendix 3

COLONEL JONATHAN EDDY

The town of Eddington received its name to honor one of its most important residents - Colonel Jonathan Eddy. Jonathan Eddy was born in 1726 in Norton (Bristol County), Massachusetts. After the Treaty of Paris in 1763, when Great Britain took control of the Province of Quebec and Nova Scotia, Jonathan Eddy decided to accept the offer of land in this former French controlled area. He left Massachusetts to settle in Chignecto Bay, where he became the Sheriff and resided there for ten years. Colonel Eddy fled Nova Scotia (along with Rev. Seth Noble and others) in 1776 and joined Colonel John Allan in Machias to enlist with his regiment of volunteers. The General Court of Massachusetts granted Col. Eddy and 19 others, 9000 acres on June 14, 1785 in the present town of Eddington. Colonel Eddy was also empowered by the General Court of Massachusetts in 1791 to issue a warrant to the new town to "meet at some convenient time and place to chuse (sic) all such Officers and towns are by law required to chuse in the month of March or April annually."

His descendants erected a large granite monument in 1892 on the exact site of Colonel Jonathan Eddy's home, with the following words:

Jonathan Eddy

1726   1804

A Captain in the French and Indian War
A Colonel in the Revolutionary War
A Representative to the Mass. General Court - 1783
First Magistrate on the Penobscot River

This town of Eddington named in his honor and part of the original grant to himself and other soldiers.

This memorial erected by his descents in 1892.

Appendix 3

Mistaken engraving of Colonel Jonathan Eddy [51, p. 334]
(see p. 150 for explanation)

Appendix 3

Portrait of Jonathan Eddy (1811-1865), great grandson of
Col. Jonathan Eddy, collection of Dr. Robert Eddy, Camden, Maine

In May of 2007, I met with Dr. Robert Eddy, great x 4 grandson of Col. Jonathan Eddy (1726-1804) in his home in Camden, Maine and was given new information regarding the engraving of his ancestor in the 1882 *History of Penobscot County*. The above Eddy Family Portrait is of Col. Jonathan Eddy's great grandson, Jonathan Eddy (1811-1865), who was said to resemble his famous ancestor and was given the name "Colonel" in deference to his famous great grandfather. A traveling portrait artist did the above portrait in the 1850's. This information was passed down to Dr. Robert Eddy from his grandfather, Frederick A. Eddy, who was born in 1847 and recorded this information for his descendants in the family copy of the 1882 *History of Penobscot County*.

Appendix 3

Petition to the Massachusetts General Court from Seth Noble,
Bangor August 24, 1796, requesting land on which to build his church,
Verification of his installment in 1786 given by Jonathan Eddy and John Brewer

Bangor Aug. 24. 1796.

To the Honourable the Senate; and House of Representatives in General Court assembled,

The Petition of Seth Noble humbly sheweth, that on the tenth Day of September 1786. he was regularly installed over the Church and Congregation in Kenduskeag Plantation, now incorporated by the name of Bangor. — This Honourable Court hath made a donation of 320 Acres of Land in each Town in the Province of Main, situated between the Rivers Kennebeck and Penobscot to the first settled Minister of the Gospel; but the peculiar situation of this Town hath prevented your Petitioner from obtaining Sd. donation for about ten Years past, greatly to his damage.

Your Petitioner humbly prays Your Honours would consider his singular situation, and issue an order to some Gentleman, to say where Sd. Lot shall be, and to lay it out. The front range is wholly settled, your Petitioner is willing to take his Land in the second range, directly back of where he now lives. At least nine tenths of Sd. Lot thus situated will fall within your Lands lately purchased of the Indians: and Your Petitioner as in duty bound shall ever pray.

Seth Noble

Bangor august 12. 1796.
These may certify whom it may concern, that the Revd. Seth Noble was regularly installed over the Church, and Congregation in this place on the tenth Day of September 1786.

Jonathan Eddy
John Brewer

Appendix 3
1767 Map of Nova Scotia showing Sunbury County and Maugerville

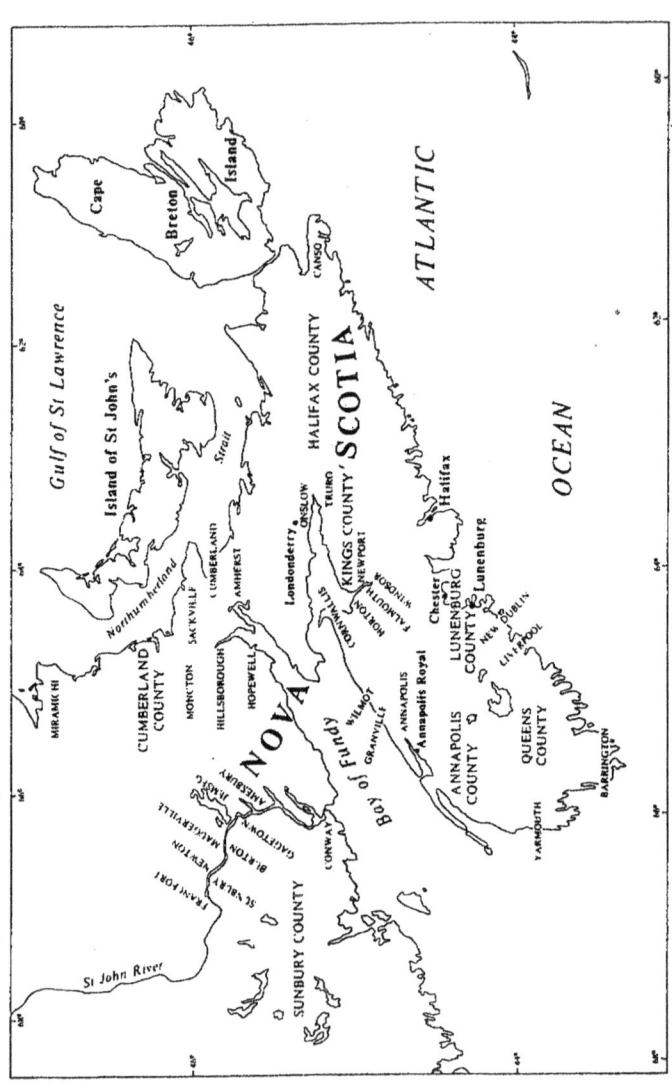

Nova Scotia 1767

Appendix 3
Map of the District of Maine, by Osgood Carleton 1795

Appendix 3

1779 Penobscot Bay at the time of the Failed Penobscot Expedition

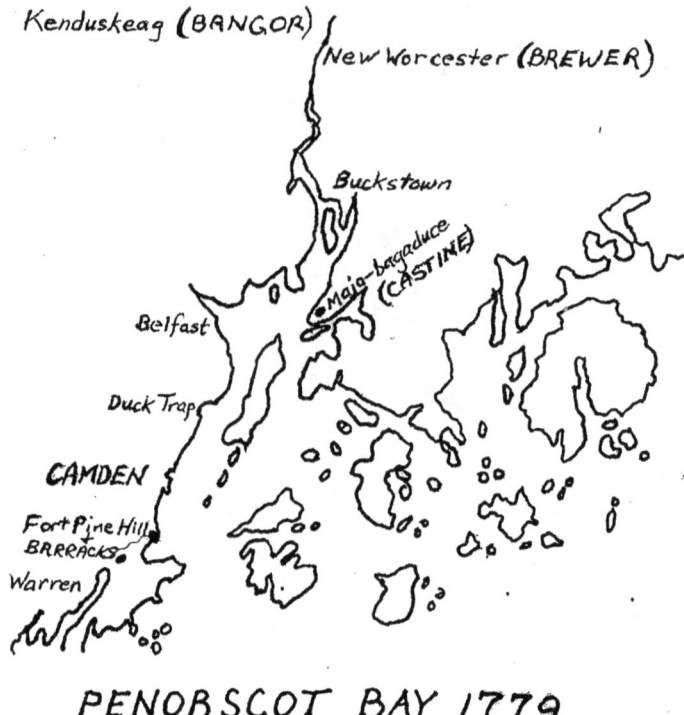

Appendix 3   155

1801 Park Holland Survey of Settlers lots who settled prior to 1798
Seth Noble, Lot 15

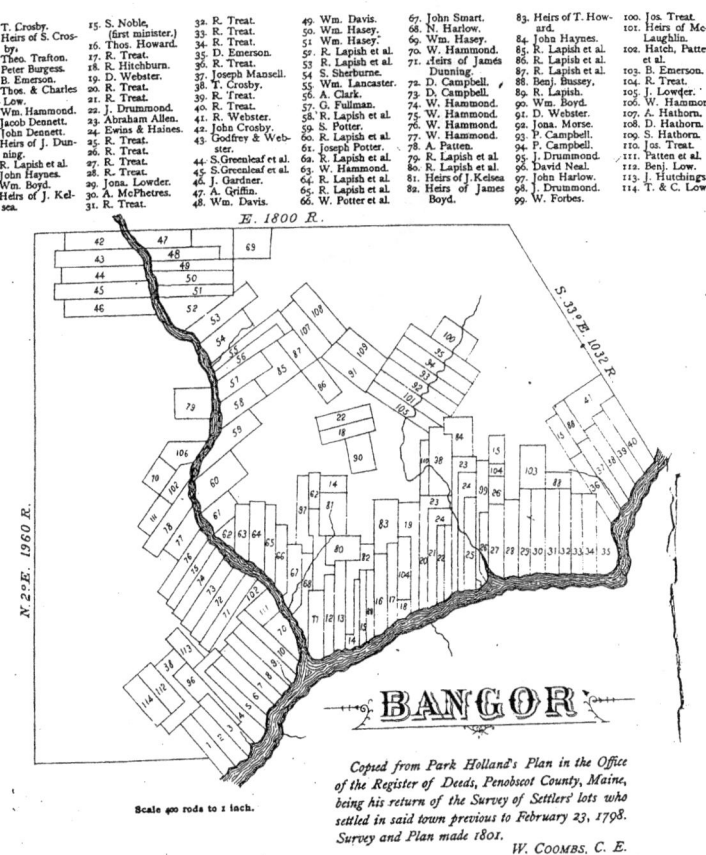

1. T. Crosby.
2. Heirs of S. Crosby.
3. Theo. Trafton.
4. Peter Burgess.
5. B. Emerson.
6. Thos. & Charles Low.
7. Wm. Hammond.
8. Jacob Dennett.
9. John Dennett.
10. Heirs of J. Dunning.
11. R. Lapish et al.
12. John Haynes.
13. Wm. Boyd.
14. Heirs of J. Kelsea.
15. S. Noble, (first minister.)
16. Thos. Howard.
17. R. Treat.
18. R. Hitchburn.
19. D. Webster.
20. R. Treat.
21. R. Treat.
22. J. Drummond.
23. Abraham Allen.
24. Ewins & Haines.
25. R. Treat.
26. R. Treat.
27. R. Treat.
28. R. Treat.
29. Jona. Lowder.
30. A. McPhetres.
31. R. Treat.
32. R. Treat.
33. R. Treat.
34. R. Treat.
35. D. Emerson.
36. R. Treat.
37. Joseph Mansell.
38. T. Crosby.
39. R. Treat.
40. R. Treat.
41. R. Webster.
42. John Crosby.
43. Godfrey & Webster.
44. S. Greenleaf et al.
45. S. Greenleaf et al.
46. J. Gardner.
47. A. Griffin.
48. Wm. Davis.
49. Wm. Davis.
50. Wm. Hasey.
51. Wm. Hasey.
52. R. Lapish et al.
53. R. Lapish et al.
54. S. Sherburne.
55. Wm. Lancaster.
56. A. Clark.
57. G. Fullman.
58. R. Lapish et al.
59. S. Potter.
60. R. Lapish et al.
61. Joseph Potter.
62. R. Lapish et al.
63. W. Hammond.
64. R. Lapish et al.
65. R. Lapish et al.
66. W. Potter et al.
67. John Smart.
68. N. Harlow.
69. Wm. Hasey.
70. W. Hammond.
71. Heirs of James Dunning.
72. D. Campbell.
73. D. Campbell.
74. W. Hammond.
75. W. Hammond.
76. W. Hammond.
77. W. Hammond.
78. A. Patten.
79. R. Lapish et al.
80. R. Lapish et al.
81. Heirs of J. Kelsea
82. Heirs of James Boyd.
83. Heirs of T. Howard.
84. John Haynes.
85. R. Lapish et al.
86. R. Lapish et al.
87. R. Lapish et al.
88. Benj. Bussey.
89. R. Lapish.
90. Wm. Boyd.
91. D. Webster.
92. Jona. Morse.
93. P. Campbell.
94. P. Campbell.
95. J. Drummond.
96. David Neal.
97. John Harlow.
98. J. Drummond.
99. W. Forbes.
100. Jos. Treat.
101. Heirs of McLaughlin.
102. Hatch, Patten, et al.
103. B. Emerson.
104. R. Treat.
105. J. Lowder.
106. W. Hammond.
107. A. Hathorn.
108. D. Hathorn.
109. S. Hathorn.
110. Jos. Treat.
111. Patten et al.
112. Benj. Low.
113. J. Hutchings.
114. T. & C. Low.

Copied from Park Holland's Plan in the Office of the Register of Deeds, Penobscot County, Maine, being his return of the Survey of Settlers' lots who settled in said town previous to February 23, 1798. Survey and Plan made 1801.

W. COOMBS, C. E.

Scale 400 rods to 1 inch.

Appendix 3
1801 Survey Map of Refugee Land in Franklinton, Ohio

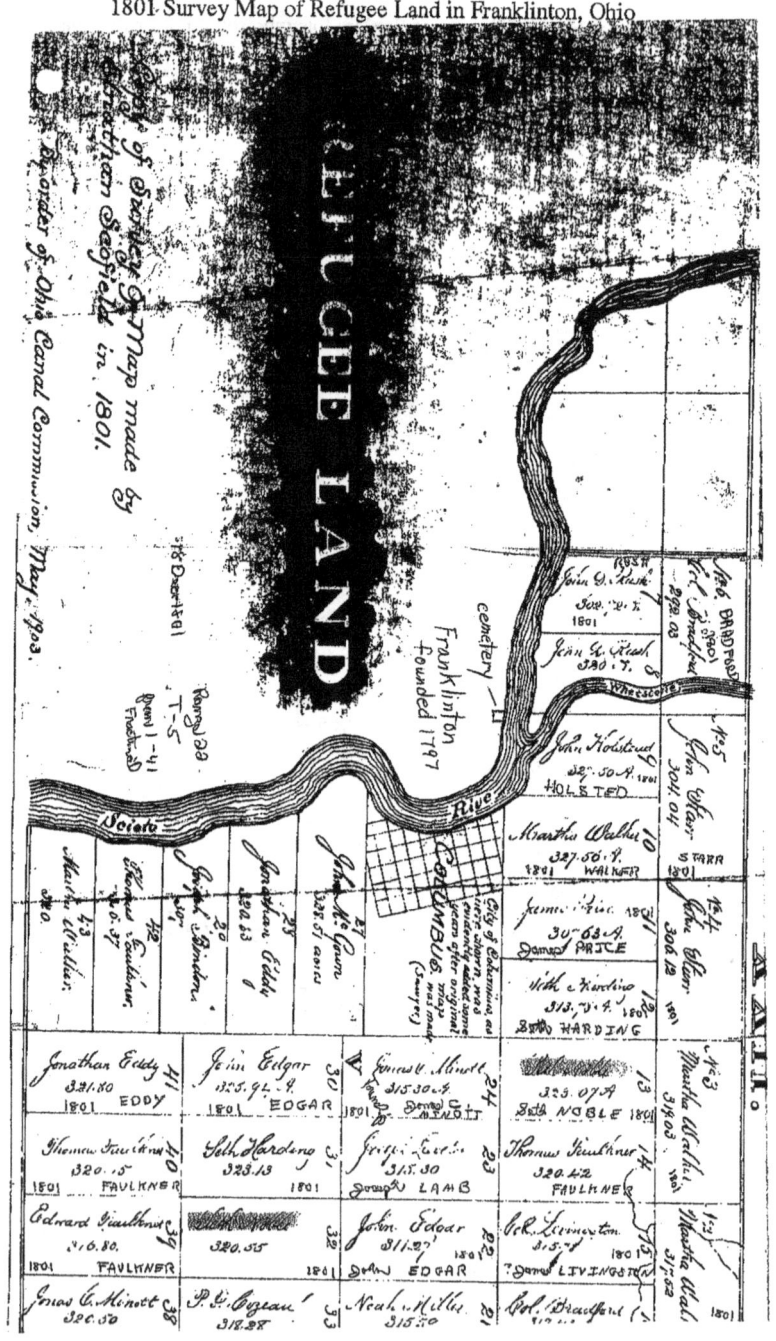

Appendix 3

1803 Map, Franklin County, Ohio

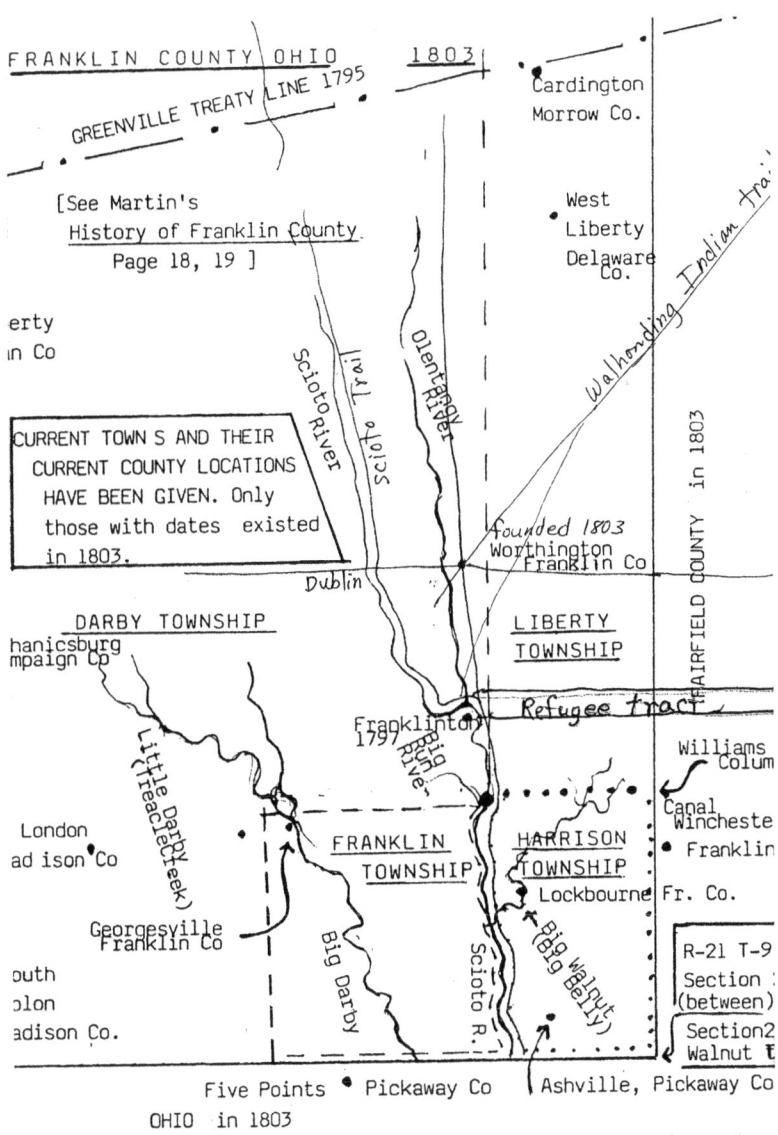

Appendix 3

1802 Seth Noble Ohio Land Grant, 320 acres, by President Thomas Jefferson and Sec. of State, James Madison

THOMAS JEFFERSON, President of the United States of America,

TO ALL TO WHOM THESE PRESENTS SHALL COME, GREETING:

Know Ye, That in pursuance of the act of Congress passed on the eighteenth day of February, 1801, entitled "An act regulating the grants of Land appropriated for the Refugees from the British Provinces of Canada and Nova Scotia," there is granted unto Seth Noble, — a certain tract of land estimated to contain Three Hundred Twenty Acres and Fifty Five Perches, being Lot Half Section Number Thirty Two West in Township Number Five and Range Twenty Two of the Lands set apart and reserved for the purpose of the claims of the Refugees aforesaid and — surveyed and located in pursuance of the act above recited: **To Have and to Hold** the said described tract of land, with the appurtenances thereof unto the said Seth Noble — and to his heirs and assigns forever, subject to the conditions, restrictions and provisions contained in the said recited act.

IN WITNESS WHEREOF, the said THOMAS JEFFERSON, President of the United States of America, hath caused the Seal of the said United States to be hereunto affixed, and signed the same with his hand, at the City of Washington, the Thirteenth Day of February — in the Year of our Lord 1802, and of the Independence of the United States of America, the Twenty Sixth.

Th. Jefferson.

By the President,

James Madison, Secretary of State.

Appendix 3

1802 Second Ohio Land Grant to Seth Noble, 323 acres, by President Thomas Jefferson and Sec. of State, James Madison

THOMAS JEFFERSON, President of the United States of America,

TO ALL, TO WHOM THESE PRESENTS SHALL COME, GREETING:

𝕶𝖓𝖔𝖜 𝖄𝖊, That in pursuance of the act of Congress passed on the eighteenth day of February, 1801, entitled "An act regulating the grants of Land appropriated for the Refugees from the British Provinces of Canada and Nova Scotia," there is granted unto Seth Noble, — a certain tract of land estimated to contain Three Hundred Twenty Three Acres and Seven Tenths, being the half section Number Thirteen West in Township Number Five and Range Twenty Two of the Lands set apart and reserved for the purpose of satisfying the claims of the Refugees aforesaid and — surveyed and located in pursuance of the act above recited: To have and to hold the said described tract of land, with the appurtenances thereof unto the said Seth Noble — and to his heirs and assigns forever, subject to the conditions, restrictions and provisions contained in the said recited act.

IN WITNESS WHEREOF, the said THOMAS JEFFERSON, President of the United States of America, hath caused the Seal of the said United States to be hereunto affixed, and signed the same with his hand, at the City of Washington, the Thirteenth Day of February — in the Year of our Lord 1802, and of the Independence of the United States of America, the Twenty sixth —

Th: Jefferson.

By the President,

James Madison, Secretary of State.

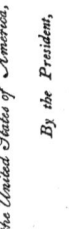

Appendix 3

Bangor City Hall, Sept. 22, 2003, "Rev. Seth Noble" and Descendants for presentation ceremony of 1791 Incorporation Charter

Appendix 3

Bangor's Recognition and Acceptance of the 1791 Original Charter
Carried by Reverend Seth Noble to the General Court of the
Commonwealth of Massachusetts
Bangor City Council **Proclamation**
22nd day of September, 2003

Recognizing Carol B. Smith Fisher

WHEREAS, Carol B. Smith Fisher, born in Bangor, has long held an interest in Bangor and its history; and

WHEREAS, in June of 2002, an enthusiastic Mrs. Fisher contacted the City Manager's Office indicating she had obtained an actual copy of Bangor's 1791 Charter signed by John Hancock; and

WHEREAS, the 1790 petition to incorporate a town by the name of Bangor was carried by Reverend Seth Noble to the General Court of the Commonwealth of Massachusetts; and

WHEREAS, further research by Mrs. Fisher brought her in contact with descendents of Reverend Seth Noble who made special arrangements for a trip to Bangor on this occasion; and

WHEREAS, this recently discovered original Charter for the Incorporation of Bangor has never been seen in Bangor before.

NOW, THEREFORE, I, NICHI S. FARNHAM, MAYOR OF THE CITY OF BANGOR, on behalf of the City Council and citizens of Bangor, do hereby recognize Carol B. Smith Fisher and express appreciation for her dedication to Bangor and its history and her perseverance in returning a copy of the 212 year old original Bangor Charter to its home.

Given this the 22nd day of September, 2003.

Nichi S. Farnham

Mayor Nichi S. Farnham

Appendix 3

Rev. Seth Noble (Kenneth P. Fisher), Sept. 22, 2003, photo taken in front of exact site of his 1794 church, Brewer, Maine

Appendix 3

Hannah (Noble) Beach (1789-1854),
daughter of Rev. Seth and Hannah (Barker) Noble

Appendix 3

Harry Gordon Noble, 1901 photo,
Great Grandson of Rev. Seth and Hannah (Barker) Noble

Appendix 3

Ambassador John Joseph Noble,
Great, Great, Great Grandson of Rev. Seth and Hannah (Barker) Noble

Appendix 3

Church of First Minister Rev. Seth Noble
United Church of Canada, formerly the Congregational Church of Maugerville
(moved to Sheffield, Sunbury County, New Brunswick, Canada)

Appendix 3

Plaque commemorating the church of Rev. Seth Noble,
First built in 1775 in Maugerville, Sunbury County, Nova Scotia

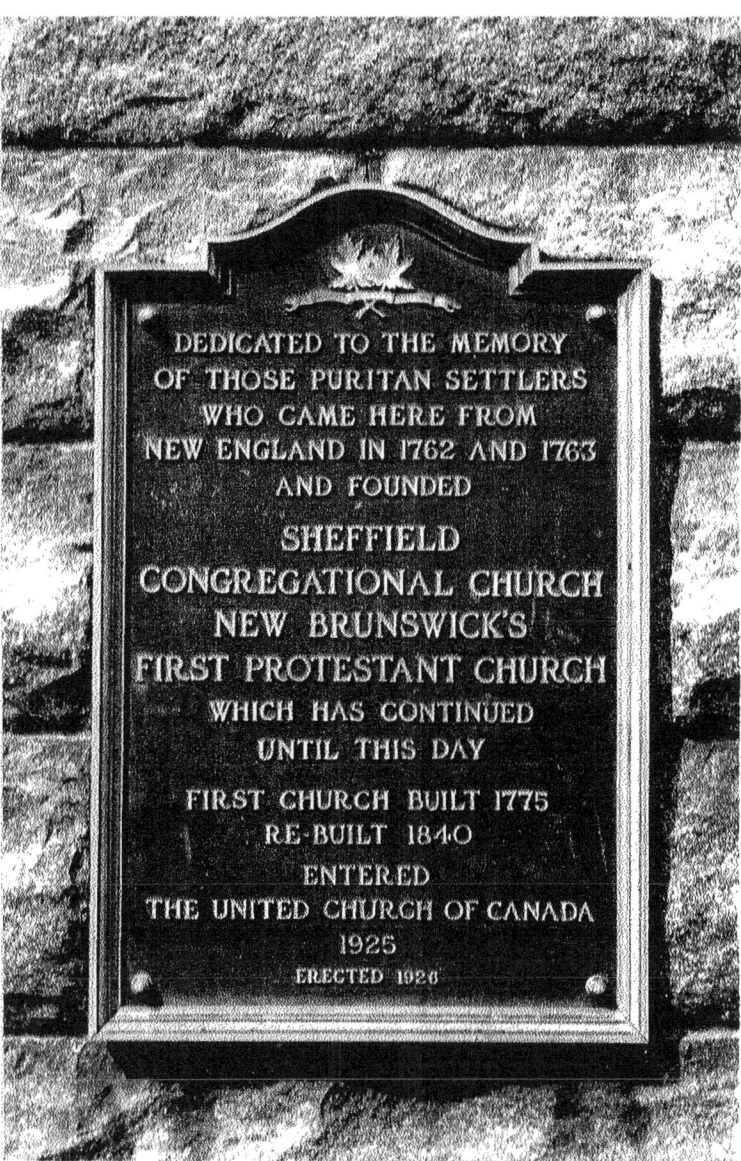

Appendix 3

Log Cabin, Maine Forest & Logging Museum, Inc, Leonard's Mills, Bradley, Maine

Appendix 3   169

1771 Home of Colonel John and Martha Brewer, Brewer, Maine
Seth and Hannah, Seth, Jr., Joseph, and Sarah Noble arrived here in 1786.

Appendix 3

Original Early Headstone of Col. John Brewer, Founder of Brewer, Maine, and Friend of Rev. Seth Noble (Oak Hill Cemetery, Brewer)

Appendix 3

Model of Two-Masted Topsail Schooner resembling the Bangor Built
SUSANNAH

Appendix 3

Headstone of Robert Hichborn, Sr., father of Susan and Eliza Hichborn and owner of the SUSANNAH, shipwrecked Oct. 18, 1798 Cape Jellison Cemetery, Stockton Springs, Maine

Appendix 3

Seth Noble's Bangor and Penobscot River 218 years later

174 Appendix 3

Seth Noble's Franklinton (Columbus), Ohio and Scioto River 202 years later

Appendix 3

175

NOBLE STREET, site of land and log cabin of Seth Noble
Franklinton (Columbus), Ohio

Brief Noble Family Genealogy

First Generation
  Thomas Noble came to Westfield, Hampden County, Massachusetts Bay Colony in the 17th century from England.

Second Generation
  Deacon Thomas Noble (son of Thomas) m. Elisabeth Dewey, Dec. 19, 1695. She was the daughter of Thomas and Constant (Hawes) Dewey. She died in Westfield, Oct. 2, 1757 at the age of 80. Deacon Thomas Noble was a farmer and built the home Seth Noble grew up in. It was located, until recently, 2 ½ miles east of the center of Westfield.

Children born in Westfield

1. *Thomas*, b. Sept. 10, 1696, m. (1) S. Root, (2) S. Belding.
2. Job, b. Jan. 28, 1699, d. June 25, 1699 (age 5 months).
3. Jonathan, b. May 1, 1700, d. Nov. 1719, (age 19).
4. Seth, b. Oct. 30, 1702, d. Dec. 4, 1702 (age 1 month).
5. Israel, b. Sept. 20, 1703, m. (1) M. Weller, (2) E. Miller.
6. Elizabeth, b. Jan. 3, 1706, m. John Shepard.
7. Lois, b. July 4, 1708, m. Josiah Keep.
8. Ebenezer, b. Oct. 11, 1711, m. Abigail Palmer.
9. Thankful, b. May 31, 1714.
10. Anna, b. Oct. 30, 1716, m. John Leonard.
11. Jonathan, b. May 23, 1721, m. Elizabeth Andrus.

Third Generation
  Thomas Noble (son of Thomas, son of Thomas), b. Sept. 10, 1696 and d. in Westfield on Feb. 8, 1776 at age 78. He was a farmer and resided in his father's homestead in Westfield. He m. **(1) *Sarah Root*** on Sept. 1, 1722 in Westfield. She d. July 19, 1760, age 59 and is buried in Westfield. (Seth Noble was their youngest child and was 17 years old when his mother died.) He m. (2) Mrs. Sarah (Field) Belding in 1761 of Hatfield, d. in Westfield Aug. 17, 1763 age 62.

Brief Noble Family Genealogy

Fourth generation

Children born in Westfield

1. Sarah, b. Aug. 11, 1723, m. Aaron Dewey.
2. Thomas, b. Feb. 6, 1725, m. Susanna Cole.
3. Stephen, b. April 16, 1727, m. Ruth Church.
4. Eunice, b. Mar. 9 1729, m. Feb. 7, 1750, Dr. Samuel Smith of Westfield. They had a child, Eunice, b. Aug. 20 1750, d. at age 21. Dr. Smith d. Aug. 6, 1794 at the age of 69.
5. John, b. Sept. 7, 1731, m. Lois Sexton.
6. Silas, b. Aug. 28, 1733, m. (1) B. Dewey; (2) M. Taylor.
7. Aaron, b. Dec. 24, 1735, served in the French and Indian Wars and d. unmarried in Westfield, Nov. 26, 1760 at the age of 24. Rev. John Ballantine of Westfield, in his diary, under the date of Nov. 27, 1760, makes the following entry:

Attended the funeral of Aaron Noble, who died of small-pox, age 25. He had served his country in 4 campaigns, had just returned from Quebec in good health, began to be sick in about one hour after his arrival and died in a week.

8. Elizabeth, b. Feb. 2, 1738, m. (1) M. Dewey, (2) J. C. Miller (3) B. Saxton.
9. Caleb, b. April, 1741, m. Mercy Kellogg of Sheffield, MA. He served in the Revolutionary War and later moved to Ohio after his wife died in 1819.
10. **Seth, b. April 15, 1743**, m. in Maugerville, Nov. 30, 1775 **(1) Hannah Barker (b. Feb. 19, 1759** in Rowley, MA, **d. June 16, 1790 in Bangor;)** m. April 11, 1793 in Orrington, District of Maine **(2) Mrs. Ruhama Emery** (widow of James Emery, who drowned in the Penobscot River on Sept. 15, 1792 and is buried in the Old Settlers Cem. in Hampden), **Ruhama d. Nov. 1805** in Montgomery, MA and is buried in the Pitcher Street Cem. With a headstone marked R. N. 1805; m. Dec. 3, 1806 in Franklinton (Columbus), Ohio **(3) Mrs. Margaret (Mary) Riddle** (widow of Magill Riddle?). **Rev. Seth Noble, d. in Franklinton (Columbus) on Sept. 15, 1807, age 64, in his log cabin on what is today NOBLE Street**. Mrs. Margaret Mary (Riddle) Noble was reported to have died shortly after Seth, but no record of her death has been found.

Brief Noble Family Genealogy

Fourth Generation

SETH NOBLE (son of Thomas, son of Thomas, son of Thomas) met (1) **Hannah Barker** in Maugerville, Sunbury County, Nova Scotia (New Brunswick after 1784), **m. Nov. 30, 1775** in Maugerville. She was **b. in Rowley, MA** to Joseph and Sarah (Palmer) Barker, **Feb. 19, 1759**. Hannah moved to Sunbury County with her parents at age 6 years. Her father was influential in the newly formed community. Nothing is known of her personal appearance except that she had blue eyes. She was reported to have been home schooled and wrote beautiful letters to Seth during their separation throughout the Revolutionary War. Hannah d. in the Kenduskeag Plantation (Bangor) while Seth was in Boston to procure an act of incorporation for Bangor. She was most probably buried near their home on State Street near the site of the current Hose 5 Fire Museum, 247 State St., Bangor.

Fifth Generation and Sixth Generation:

Children by Seth and Hannah (Barker) Noble

1. **Seth, Jr.,** (son of Seth, son of Thomas, son of Thomas, son of Thomas), b. Aug. 5, 1777, in Sheffield, Nova Scotia (New Brunswick), d. at the age of 21, when the schooner SUSANNAH from Bangor to Boston was lost at sea during a snowstorm and was reported to have hit rocks off Boon Island, on Oct. 18, 1798. All souls were lost and many belongings washed up on shore at Halibut Point, Cape Ann, MA. A trunk marked S. Noble, Jr. was retrieved by his father. He was reported to have been universally loved by all who knew him. [See Chapter Six and Appendix 2 for the extensive research done on this important vessel.]

2. **Joseph,** (son of Seth, son of Thomas, son of Thomas, son of Thomas), b. June 13, 1783, in Newmarket, NH; m. Mary Ackerson (b. Sept. 23, 1794 in Sheffield, Sunbury County, NB, d. Aug 2. 1864 in Brighton, Carleton County, NB), June 9, 1812, he d. Feb. 26, 1869, age 86, Becaguimec, Carleton, Co., NB. His mother died when he was 7 years old and was brought in 1791 by his father to live with his mother's brother in Maugerville, with his 3-year-old younger brother Benjamin. Seth Noble was forced to

separate these two boys from the rest of the family so that they could receive schooling that was not yet present in Bangor. These two boys were raised by the Barker family and never saw their father again. His uncle, Benjamin Barker, raised Joseph.

Children of Joseph and Mary (Ackerson) Noble were:

(Grandchildren of Rev. Seth and Hannah (Barker) Noble)

    a. Sophia Jane Noble, b. Feb. 9, 1814, Brighton, NB, d. May 27, 1862, Woodstock, NB.
    b. Mary Ann Noble, b. Sept. 3, 1815, Brighton, NB, d. Jan. 19, 1895, Rockland, Carleton, County, NB
    c. Seth Noble, b. Dec. 14, 1817, d. Fredericton, York, County, NB
    d. Sarah Noble, b. July 16, 1820, Brighton, NB, d. Dec. 1, 1861, Upper Brighton, NB
    e. Elijah Noble, b. Aug. 28, 1822, Brighton, NB, d. before 1861.
    f. Lettia Noble, b. July 22, 1824, Lower Brighton, NB, d. July 31, 1920, Upper Woodstock, NB
    g. Joel Noble, b. July 26, 1826, Lower Brighton, NB,
    h. Benjamin B. Noble, b. June 23, 1828, Lower Brighton, NB
    i. Hannah Noble, b. May 22, 1831, Lower Brighton, NB, d. Jan. 25, 1856, buried in Old Calvanist Baptist Cemetery, Rockland, NB

3. **Sarah**, (dau. of Seth, son of Thomas, son of Thomas, son of Thomas), b. June 1, 1785, in Hallowell, District of Maine, m. Martin Bartholomew on Nov. 4, 1804 (he was born Aug. 18, 1776 in Harwinton, CT and d. Mar. 13, 1842 in Washington, D.C.) Martin Bartholomew was the first captain of the first steamboat ever built; the **ROBERT FULTON.** His father Andrew was a Captain in the Revolutionary War. Sarah d. Nov. 15, 1836, age 51 in Montgomery, MA, and is buried in the Pitcher Street Cemetery in Montgomery.

Brief Noble Family Genealogy

Children of Sarah Noble and Martin Bartholomew:

(Grandchildren of Seth and Hannah (Barker) Noble)

    a. Albert Martin Bartholomew, b. Feb. 6, 1805, Montgomery, MA
    b. Marilla Bartholomew, b. July 20, 1806, d. Oct. 16, 1874, Westfield, MA
    c. Andrew Bartholomew, b. Nov. 13, 1808, Columbus, Ohio, d. Feb. 6, 1852, St. Louis, Missouri
    d. Maria Bartholomew, Nov. 27, 1810, Columbus, Ohio
    e. Eliza Ann Bartholomew, b. Oct. 7, 1813, Columbus, Ohio, d. May 1, 1875, Fall River MA, m. Silas Bushnell, Sept. 27, 1838, Granville,Ohio
    f. Mary Bartholomew, b. June 18, 1817, d. Feb. 2, 1859, Waverly, Ohio, m. Rufus Fosdick Graves, May 8, 1838
    g. Caroline Elizabeth Bartholomew, b. June 12, 1819, Montgomery, MA, d. June 24, 1876, Granville, Ohio, m. James Willard Fosdick

4. **Benjamin** (son of Seth, son of Thomas, son of Thomas, son of Thomas), b. June 25, 1787 in Kenduskeag Plantation (Bangor) m. Mar. 29, 1810 (1) Susanna Currier (d. Dec. 18, 1841 in Brighton, Carleton, Co., NB); m. Mar. 15, 1845 (2) Christiana McMullen Buber (d. Jan. 24, 1860 in Brighton, NB); Benjamin d. April 12, 1860, age 73, in Lower Brighton, NB. Brought to Maugerville, Sunbury County, NB in 1791 with his brother Joseph and was brought up by uncle Joseph Barker, Hannah (Barker) Noble's brother. He was a farmer, blacksmith, Justice of the Peace, and Postmaster.

Children of Benjamin and Susanna (Currier) Noble:

(Grandchildren of Seth and Hannah (Barker) Noble)
    a. Theodore Harding Noble, b. Sept. 25, 1820, Brighton, Carleton Co., NB, d. Oct. 2, 1898, Bristol, NB

Brief Noble Family Genealogy

    b. Hannah Barker Noble, b. Dec. 30, 1810, d. 1877, Bridgewater, Maine
    c. George Seth Noble, b. Jan. 15, 1812, Sheffield, NB, d. April 19, 1891
    d. Enoch Barker Noble, b. April 17, 1818, d. Blaine, Maine
    e. Joseph Barker Noble, b. Aug 4, 1815, Brighton, NB, d. Mar. 4, 1909, Woodstock, NB, lived to become the oldest Baptist minister in North America
    f. Rebecca Noble, b. May 13, 1823, Brighton, NB, d. 1919, Brighton, NB
    g. Issachar Currier Noble, b. Dec. 25, 1825, Brighton, NB, d. Sept. 30, 1872, Hodgdon, Maine
    h. David Duncan Noble, b. Feb. 1, 1828, Brighton
    i. Elizabeth (Eliza) Ann Noble, b. Aug. 7, 1831, Brighton, NB, d. 1916

5. **Hannah** (dau. of Seth, son of Thomas, son of Thomas, son of Thomas), b. Sept. 11, 1789, in Kenduskeag Plantation (Bangor), m. (1) N. Gorham, (2) U. Beach, (3) C. Twiford; Hannah d. Nov. 17, 1854, age 65, in Amity, Madison County, Ohio. A touching epitaph on her headstone states, "daughter of Rev. Seth Noble."

Children of Hannah Noble and Nathan Gorham:

(Grandchildren of Seth and Hannah (Barker) Noble)

    a. Elizabeth Gorham, b. Mar. 29, 1808, Montgomery, MA, d. Feb. 16, 1837, Darby Plains, Ohio
    b. Belinda Gorham, b. Oct. 25, 1811

Children of Hannah Noble and Uri Beach:

(Grandchildren of Seth and Hannah (Barker) Noble)

    c. Elizabeth Beach, b. May 25, 1817, Amity, Madison County, Ohio
    d. Mary Beach, b. April 19, 1819, Amity, Ohio

Brief Noble Family Genealogy 183

    e. Hannah Noble Beach, b. Feb. 5, 1821, Amity, Ohio
    f. Malona Case Beach, b. April 17, 1823, Amity, Ohio
    g. Uri Beach, b. Jan. 13, 1826
    h. John Noble Beach, b. Jan. 27, 1829, Canaan, Ohio
    i. William Morrow Beach, b. May 10, 1831, Canaan, Ohio

Children of Seth and Ruhama Noble

6. **Betsey** (dau. of Seth, son of Thomas, son of Thomas, son of Thomas), b. Nov. 23, 1793, in Bangor, m. James Phillips, Jan. 10, 1808 (b. Aug. 22, 1776 in Philadelphia, PA, d. Aug. 4, 1823 in Alexander Co., Illinois); Betsey d. Sept. 2, 1850 in Clear Creek, Alexander Co., Illinois.

    Children of Betsey Noble and James Phillips
    (Grandchildren of Seth and Ruhama Noble)

        a. Thomas Noble Phillips, b. July 8, 1809, d. Mar. 29, 1829
        b. Samuel Phillips, b. Sept. 7, 1811, d. Oct. 30, 1811
        c. Martha Phillips, b. May 9, 1813, d. Mar. 20, 1842; m. William C. McMillen
        d. Amos Garrel Phillips, b. Mar. 7, 1816, d. Jan. 31, 1868, Clear Creek Landing, Illinois; m. Mary R. Brown, April 16, 1846
        e. Samuel Miller Phillips, b. Aug 3. 1818, d. Mar. 28, 1842; m. Susan Wright, Jan. 15, 1839
        f. Mary Phillips, b. Feb. 25, 1821, d. Sept. 2, 1822
        g. James Phillips, b. Jan. 8, 1824, d. July 28, 1853; m. Martha Bankstone, Feb. 9, 1847

7. **Thomas** (son of Seth, son of Thomas, son of Thomas, son of Thomas), b. July 28, 1795 in Bangor, d. July 31, 1795

8. **Polly** (dau. of Seth, son of Thomas, son of Thomas, son of Thomas), b. Sept. 26, 1796 in Bangor, m. Elisha Atkins, Nov. 25, 1816, d. Pleasant Valley, Porter Co., Ohio

Brief Noble Family Genealogy

Children of Polly Noble and Elisha Atkins:

(Grandchildren of Seth and Ruhama Noble)

    a. Azubah Barnes Atkins, b. Apr. 17, 1818, d. Feb. 15, 1821
    b. Lyman Atkins, b. Aug. 26, 1819
    c. Seth Noble Atkins, b. July 8, 182, Montgomery, MA, d. Jan. 14, 1823, Montgomery, MA
    d. Martin Bartholomew Atkins, b. Aug 11, 1823, Westfield, MA, d. Aug. 13, 1826, Westfield, MA
    e. Laura Ann Atkins, b. Mar. 28, 1826, Westfield, MA, d. July 17, 1849, Morgan Township, Porter, County, Illinois; m. Andrew Jackson Wright, Dec. 1846
    f. Franklin Atkins, b. June 5, 1828, Westfield, MA; m. Elouisa Van Dalsem, Sept., 1851
    g. Henry Rollin Atkins, b. Jan. 5, 1830, Pierpoint, Ohio, d. Aug. 16, 1841, Pierpoint, Ohio
    h. Clinton Gould Atkins, b. Aug 18, 1836, Pierpoint, Ohio, d. 1862, Arkansas

9. **John Adams** (son of Seth, son of Thomas, son of Thomas, son of Thomas), b. April 18, 1799 in New Market, NH, d. Aug. 21, 1819, age 20;

Money being scarce in his neighborhood of his residence, he started with a party of young men for Sandusky, Ohio, where labor was in demand and money abundant. They all, thirty in number, took the typhoid fever, and but one recovered. Young Noble was able to reach his friends, and d. universally beloved, unm., near Worthington, Ohio [2, p. 212].

The majority of this Noble Family genealogy came from the excellent work of Lucius M. Boltwood in his 1878 *History and Genealogy of the Family of Thomas Noble* [12]. Further records are from Orrington and Hampden, Maine vital records and early Franklinton (Columbus), Ohio vital records. Many thanks to John Joseph Noble, descendant of Benjamin Noble, for further information on the children and grandchildren of Seth Noble.

Acknowledgments

When I first considered doing research into the life of Rev. Seth Noble, I could not have imagined the amount of material and documents I would eventually uncover. At times I felt as if I were reliving a nursery rhyme with breadcrumbs spread along the path for me to follow. Slowly the pieces started to come together to tell a story quite different from the version to which Bangor still clings.

This book would not have come to fruition without the love and support of my husband, Chicago born and University of Chicago graduate, Kenneth Paul Fisher. He has been my editor and mentor and has spent countless hours in reading and re-reading my manuscript for clarity, punctuation and style. Without his extensive knowledge of the Bible, English skills, editing ability and his own *Chicago Manual of Style*, this work would have remained only a figment of my imagination.

Next on my list of people who made this book possible were the many descendants of Rev. Seth Noble who all grew up knowing they were related to someone very special. Their support for my work was invaluable. The "Noble Ladies" as I refer to them, drove all the way to Maine from New York for the recognition of their ancestor's naming of Bangor. Descendant Joanne Schotthoefer not only located her ancestor's early sermon at the Andover-Harvard Theological Library, she honored her ancestor by performing the hymn tune BANGOR with the accompaniment of organist John Haskel. Twelve-year-old Murphy rang the bell to introduce her ancestor and hearken us back to the year 1791. Noble family matriarch Florence Sihksnel did her ancestor proud with her inspired presentation of the 1791 birth certificate of Bangor. She exuded the same public persona her ancestor had over 200 years prior. Their continued friendship and support has made this book a pleasure.

Ambassador John Joseph Noble, descendant of Seth and Hannah Noble's son Benjamin, not only shared all of his research with me, and wrote the wonderful foreword, but also infused the work with his enthusiasm and knowledge. John is descended from the young 4-year-old Bangor-born son whom Seth Noble brought to Canada to be raised by his in-laws after the death of his beloved Hannah. This was a heart-rending decision and sacrifice to see that his two sons receive the schooling that was not yet available in Bangor. John Joseph Noble is the proof that Seth Noble's horrendous sacrifice was not made in vain. Thank you, John!

My dear friend, Ann French Flewelling, not only shared her knowledge of early Canadian and Maine history, she was a constant moral guide to the completion of this work. She stayed with me through every step of the way and was a constant source of inspiration. Being able to share this hard-fought research with someone who understands its importance was an immeasurable asset.

Robert C. Brooks is one of those rare individuals you meet once in a lifetime. His knowledge of this time period and his nautical expertise were so compelling that a conversation with him is like a walk back in time. His many letters and phone conversations regarding the shipwrecked SUSANNAH are a treasured memory, and his shared knowledge and expertise gave me the courage to write on this important tragedy.

Philip Mead is a Harvard University Ph.D. candidate and expert on the American Revolution. He has done extensive work on the biography of that famous soldier of the Revolution, Joseph Plumb Martin (1760-1850). He was able to answer my many questions on material culture of this time period and prevented me from making a serious mistake in the life of Seth Noble. Published in the *Bangor Centennial Celebration* in 1870, was a poem attributed to Rev. Seth Noble at the time of his wife's eulogy. The name of this poem was "Sophronia." I had tried repeatedly to learn who Sophronia was and I had all but given up, when Philip solved this mystery for me.

My research into old Protestant hymn tunes was given a great boost by the willingness of Professor Wyn Thomas of the School of Music, University of Wales (Bangor, Wales) United Kingdom), to share with me his research on the hymn tune BANGOR and the life of William Tans'ur. He also provided me with a Celtic translation of the word *Bangor*, meaning *wattle*

Acknowledgments

(woven wood) fence and *(gor)* the Welsh word for choir. This name is appropriate on so many levels!

My Canadian research was greatly enhanced by the help of historian George H. Hayward and his extensive work on the early settlers of Maugerville on the St. John River of Sunbury County, New Brunswick. His photo of the church where Rev. Seth Noble first delivered his sermons is much appreciated.

My Ohio research would not have been possible without the help of the Franklin County Genealogical and Historical Society in Columbus, Ohio. Susan A. Bauer, research volunteer, did so much work researching Seth Noble's time in Ohio that my chapter on Ohio turned out to be even more than I had hoped.

In locating the burial place of Seth Noble, four people must be mentioned. Lolita Guthrie Ohio Genealogical Society Board of Trustees and Chair of the Cemetery Committee, spent much time trying to locate the burial grounds of Seth Noble, which she later discovered to be in the Old Franklinton Cemetery in Columbus.

Bea Murphy is author of the Arthur Boke story, the first known African American born in Columbus in 1803 and originally buried in the Franklinton Cemetery. Bea Murphy discovered that the cemetery bronze plaque had been stolen and reported this to Columbus City attorney, Richard Pfeiffer.

Barbara Carmen of the (Columbus) *Dispatch* picked this story up just before the 4th of July, and the question, "I wonder who Revolutionary War Solider, Seth Noble was?" led to the discovery of the Seth Noble burial place. Then a follow-up *Dispatch* article reported that the burial site of the man who named Bangor, Maine had been discovered in the Old Franklinton Cemetery in downtown Columbus. Lolita Guthrie read the first article and mailed it to me along with a large map of Columbus, and a red circle where Seth was buried. This caused a flurry of welcome information to pour in. This is an example of how long-lost information seemed miraculously to come my way.

The recording of our early history of Maine was dependent on individuals who took it upon themselves to try to document names, places, and events that took place in the far distant past. Joseph Whitcomb Porter, starting at the age of 61, published a monthly historical and genealogical magazine from 1885 to 1894, *The Bangor Historical Magazine* and then *The Maine Historical Magazine*. His effort to document Maine history was nothing short of extraordinary. Without his work over 124 years ago, this book would not have been possible.

The following libraries have all spent many hours trying to help me with my research. The Bangor Public Library in Bangor, Maine is one of the best libraries in New England, and their reference librarians were inspirational. Many thanks to the Fogler Library of the University of Maine at Orono, Maine. Also, Frances O'Donnell, curator of Manuscripts and Archives, Andover-Harvard Theological Library, Harvard Divinity School, Cambridge, Massachusetts, made it possible for me to read Rev. Seth Noble's early 1774 sermon delivered throughout Massachusetts and Canada. And finally, Elise Bernier-Feeley, reference librarian for the Forbes Library, Northampton, Massachusetts sent me a copy of a later Rev. Seth Noble sermon.

The scholars working on the *Papers of George Washington* at the University of Virginia showed great patience with my search for the letter Seth Noble wrote to George Washington in 1777. We both tried very hard to locate this letter; although it was not found, I certainly enjoyed the search.

Bill Copley of the Tuck Library, Concord, New Hampshire thankfully researched the unknown shipwreck of the SUSANNAH by searching the microfilm of the New Hampshire Gazette.

The Sandy Bay Historical Society and Museum in Rockport, Massachusetts, spent many hours helping me identify this lost shipwreck. A thank you also goes out to the Archives Committee, City of Gloucester, for searching their materials.

I spent countless hours trying to locate the Rev. Seth Noble journal. The Lucius Boltwood Papers are housed at the Jones Library in Amherst, Massachusetts and, since Mr. Boltwood quoted excerpts from this, the reference librarians poured through the Boltwood Papers in search of this journal. Even though this did not prove to be the location, I greatly appreciate the effort.

The Sunbury (Ohio) Public library shared with me the unpublished research, "Origin of the Name Sunbury," by Carleton and Dorothy Burrer.

Acknowledgments

Last but not least, I want to thank my parents, John Eldrid Smith, M.D. and Florence Irene Bishop Smith, R.N., for living in Bangor, Maine at the time of my birth. My mother was alive at the outset of this project, but sadly, she did not live to see its completion. I am sincerely grateful for her abiding love and encouragement throughout my entire life. What a delightful dream for me to imagine both Seth Noble and my mother in heaven sharing their many stories on the old State Street neighborhood! *Mikwid hamin!*

REFERENCES

1. Bangor Committee of Arrangements. *The Centennial Celebration of the Settlement of Bangor.* Sept. 30 1869, Bangor, Maine: Benjamin A. Burr, Printer, 1870.

    This book does not acknowledge Bangor's original incorporation of 1791 and chooses a centennial date from 1769 to honor the first known English colonial settler, Jacob Bussell.

2. Boltwood, Lucius M. *History and Genealogy of the Family of Thomas Noble of Westfield, Massachusetts with Genealogical Notes of other Families by the Name of Noble.* Hartford, CT: Press of Case, Lockwood & Brainard Co., 1878, pp. 202-212.

    The Boltwood Papers can be found at the Jones Library in Amherst, MA, a search for Rev. Noble's diary was conducted without success. Excellent research on Seth Noble – eleven pages!

3. Burrer, Carleton S. and Dorothy Burrer. "The Origin of the Name Sunbury." Unpublished paper from Sunbury, Ohio, 1976.

    Available in Sunbury, Ohio Public Library.

4. Chadbourne, Ava Harriett. *Maine Place Names and the Peopling of its Towns.* Portland, Maine: The Bond Wheelwright Co., 1955.

5. Cox, H. Russell, and David L. Swett. *History and Genealogy of Orrington, Maine.* Brewer, Maine: Orrington Historical Society and Cay-Bel Publishing Co., 1988.

6. Davenport, Linda. *Divine Song on the Northeast Frontier: Maine's Sacred Tunebooks, 1800-1830.* Composers of North America – No. 18. Lanham, Maryland & London: The Scarecrow Press, Inc., 1996.

    Personal Telephone Interview with Dr. Davenport on July 7, 2003.

7. Edwards, George Thornton. *Music and Musicians of Maine.* Portland, Maine: The Southworth Press, 1928.

8. *History of Franklin and Pickaway Counties, Ohio with Illustrations and Biographical Sketches, Some of the Prominent Men and Pioneers.* (1796-

References

1880), Columbus, Ohio: Williams Bros., 1888.

9. *History of Madison County Ohio*. Chicago: W. H. Beers & Co., 1883, pp. 1026-1027.

10. Kidder, Frederick. *Military Operations in Eastern Maine and Nova Scotia During the Revolution Chiefly Compiled from the Journals and Letters of Colonel John Allan, with Notes and a Memoir of Colonel John Allan.* Albany, NY: Joel Munsell, 1867, New York: Kraus Reprint Co., 1971.

11. McCutchan, Robert Guy. *Hymn Tune Names: Their Sources and Significance.* Nashville and New York: Abingdon Press, 1957.

12. Porter, Joseph W. *The Bangor Historical Magazine (later Maine Historical Magazine)*, Vol. I-Vol. IX, Bangor, Maine: Benjamin A. Burr, Printer, 1885-94, reprinted Camden, Maine: Picton Press, 1993.

   "The Early Settlement of Bangor," pp. 2-20, "Municipal History of Bangor," pp. 6-9, Rev. Seth Noble, "The First Minister of Bangor," pp. 66-69. This is a treasure trove of original documents, memoirs, vital records, ships logs, muster rolls, letters etc., pertaining to early Maine history. Every public library in Maine should have these valuable books in its collection!

13. Stewart, Gordon, and George Rawlyk. *A People Highly Favoured of God: The Nova Scotia Yankees and the American Revolution.* Toronto: Macmillan of Canada, 1972.

14. Vickery, James. "The Settlement of Old Kenduskeag." Bangor, Maine: from *Paper Talks*, Impact Publications, 1978.

15. Williamson, William D. *History of the State of Maine from Its First Discovery, AD 1602, to the Separation, AD 1820*, Vol. II., Hallowell, Maine: Glazier, Masters & Co., 1832, pp. 552 and 430-461.

   Even though there are errors in this work, this is the most complete history of Maine prior to 1832. William D. Williamson was a resident of Bangor and a one-time governor of Maine. He unfortunately did not check the Massachusetts General Court Records for the 1787 Sunbury Petition and records the old undocumented "oral history" of the founding of Bangor.

16. *Papers of George Washington*. Revolutionary War Series. Volumes 3, 11 and 12. Charlottesville: University of Virginia Press, 1988-2002.

   A complete search for Seth Noble letter was done

References

without results. Best possible source of information regarding the founding of our nation. My sincere thanks to the University of Virginia for sharing George Washington with the world!

17. Library of Congress Manuscript Dept. "The Papers of General James Grant." Microfilm for Nov. - Dec. 1776.

    These are the letters of British General James Grant of Ballindalloch Castle, Aberdeen, Scotland, discovered in 1999 and only available at the Library of Congress.

18. Clarke, Ernest. *The Siege of Fort Cumberland – 1776*. McGill-Queen Press, pp. 80-83, 1995.

19. Ahlin, John Howard. *Maine Rubicon: Downeast Settlers During the American Revolution*. Rockport, Maine: Picton Press, 1966, reprinted in 1967 and 1997.

20. *HOLY BIBLE*, King James Version. New York: Oxford University Press.

21. Sprague, John Francis. *Sprague's Journal of Maine History*. Dover, Maine: 1915.
    Available at Bangor Public Library.

22. Drisko, George W. *Narrative of the Town of Machias – the Old and the New the Early and the Late*. Machias, Maine: Press of the Republican, pp. 52-59, 1904.

23. Thomas, Wyn. Professor, School of Music, University of Wales at Bangor, U.K., Correspondence and shared research of hymn tune BANGOR, June 2003.

24. Temperly, Nicolas. , Professor, University of Illinois, author of the Hymn-Tune Index. Urbanna, IL, telephone interviews July 2003.

25. Van Dyck, Mary Louise. Coordinator of the Dictionary of American Hymnology, Oberlin College Library, Oberlin, Ohio, correspondence and telephone interview, July, 2003.

26. Watts, Isaac. *Hymns and Spiritual Songs in Three Books*. Boston: Printed by Manning and Loring, 1769.

    Available at the University of Maine, Fogler Library Microfiche #S4 no. 27476.

27. Tate and Brady. *A New Version of the Psalms of David*. Boston: 1760.

References

Available at the University of Maine, Fogler Library, Microfiche #E37619.

28. Flagg, Josiah. *A Collection of the Best Psalm Tune in two three and four parts*. Engraving done by Paul Revere, Boston: Josiah Flagg Printers, 1764.

    Available at the University of Maine, Fogler Library, Microfiche.

29. Tans'ur, William. *The American Melody Complete* Printed and published by Daniel Bayley, 7th Ed., Newbury-Port and Boston: 1771.

    A copy obtained with thanks to the Newburyport Public Library, Newburyport, MA.

30. Julian, John. *A Dictionary of Hymnology*. London: 1907.

    From the University of Wales – Bangor. Thank you to Professor Wyn Thomas!

31. *Christian Hymns*, compiled by the Evangelical Movement of Wales.

    From the University of Wales, Bangor.

32. Stulken, Marilyn Kay. *Hymnal Companion to the Lutheran Book of Worship*. Philadelphia: Fortress Press, pp. 503-504, 1981.

33. Noble, Rev. Seth. *Two Sermons Preached at Westhampton - June 26, 1802*, Northhampton, Massachusetts: Hive Office, Thomas M. Pomroy, 1804.

    Available at the University of Maine, Fogler Library, Microfiche, and a copy made for me by Special Collections at the Forbes Library in Northampton, MA.

34. Noble, Rev. Seth. "Sermon Preached in 1774 and 1775." bms 500, Andover-Harvard Theological Library, Harvard Divinity School, Cambridge, Massachusetts.

    Thanks to Seth Noble descendant, Joanne Schotthoefer, for locating this important sermon for me. (See Chapter One).

35. New Brunswick Historical Society. George H. Hayward. "Pioneer Preacher–Rev. Seth Noble" (1992); and F. A. McGrand, M.D. "A Parson Leads them to War" (Chapter 2 of *Backward Glances at Sunbury and Queens* 1971).

    Thanks to Seth Noble descendant, J.J. Noble, for the McGrand source, and to George H. Hayward.

References

36. Hannay, James. "The Maugerville Settlement, 1763-1824," Vol. One .of *Collections of the New Brunswick Historical Society*, 1894.
    Thanks to John J. Noble.

37. Barker, H.W. "The Maugerville Church and the American Revolution." *Acadiensis*. New Brunswick Genealogical Society, 1904.

    Thanks to John J. Noble.

38. Swett, David. Orrington historian and genealogist. Telephone interview regarding Seth Noble's wife Ruhama, Jan. 17, 2004.

39. Kilby, William H. *Eastport and Passamaquoddy: A Collection of Historical and Biographical Sketches*. Eastport, Maine: Edward E. Shead, 1888.

40. National Archives, Washington, D.C. Revolutionary War Pension Record. Isaac Bussell, Bangor, District of Maine, Massachusetts, 1827.

    Thank you to my dear friend Ann Flewelling for sharing this part of her Bussell family genealogy.

41. Forbes, Esther. *Paul Revere and the World He Lived In*. Boston: Houghton Mifflin Company (Cambridge, Massachusetts: The Riverside Press), 1942.
    Robert Hitchborn letter on p. 467.

42. Crouse, D. E. *The Ohio Gateway*. New York and London: Charles Scribner's Sons, 1938.

43. Hurt, R. Douglas. *The Ohio Frontier: Crucible of the Old Northwest, 1720-1830*. Bloomington, Indiana: Indiana University Press, 1996.

44. Roseboom, Eugene H. and Francis P. Weisenberger. *A History of Ohio*. Columbus: The Ohio State Archaelogical Historical Society, 1953.

45. Applebee, Robert B. "Sailing Vessels Built in the Penobscot River Towns in Maine." Unpublished manuscript, 1941.

    Available at the Penobscot Marine Museum Research Library in Searsport, Maine.

46. Hichborn, Faustina. *Historical Sketch of Stockton Springs*. Waterville, Maine: Press of Central Maine Publishing Co, 1908.

47. Bentley, D. D., Rev. William. *The Diary of William Bentley*, Volume 2, January, 1793-December, 1802. Gloucester, Massachusetts: Peter Smith, 1962.

References

48. Jameson, E. O. *The Jamesons America (1647-1900)*. Boston, Massachusetts: Genealogical Records and Memoranda, 1901.

49. Dudley, Dean. *History and Genealogy of the Bangs Family in America*. Wakefield, Massachusetts: A. W. Brownell, 1896.

50. Ellis, Alice V. *The Story of Stockton Springs, Maine*. Belfast, Maine: Kelley Press, Inc., 1955, reprinted, Brooks, Maine: The Historical Society of Stockton Springs, Little Letterpress Robin Hood Books, 1989.

51. Williams and Chase Co. *The History of Penobscot County Maine*, 1882.

    Available at the Bangor Public Library.

52. *Memorial of the 100th Anniversary of the Settlement of Dennysville, Maine*. Portland, Maine: B. Thurston and Co. Printers, 1886.

53. *The History of Frankfort, Maine – 1774-1976*. Belfast, Maine: J. A. Black Co, Printers, 1989.

54. Dwight, Margaret Van Horn. *A Journey to Ohio in 1810*. New Haven: Yale University Press, 1912.

55. Martin, William T. *History of Franklin County*. Columbus, Ohio: Follett, Foster & Company, 1858.

56. McCormick, Virginia E. "The Settling of the Refugee Lands," *The Columbus Monthly*, February 1982.

57. State Auditor, State of Ohio. *A Short History of Ohio Land Grants*.

58. Daughters of the American Revolution. State Chairman. *The Official Roster of the Soldiers of the American Revolution Buried in the State of Ohio*. compiled by the Adjutant General, Military Registrar.

59. Martin, Joseph Plumb. *Private Yankee Doodle – A Narrative of a Revolutionary Soldier: Some of the Adventures, Dangers and Sufferings of Joseph Plumb Martin*, Eastern National, reprint, 2000, originally printed in Hallowell, Maine, 1830.

    A must read for anyone interested in the American Revolution!

60. Locke, John L. *History of Camden (1605-1859)*. Hallowell, Maine: Masters, Smith & Company, 1859.

References

61. McCullough, David. *John Adams*. New York: Simon and Schuster, 2001.

62. Marshall, John. *The Life of George Washington* . . . , Vols, I-V, Fredericksburg, Virginia: The Citizens' Guild of Washington's Boyhood Home, 1926, reprint of 1804-07 edition.

63. Bancroft, D. D. *The Life of George Washington*. Vols., I-II, Boston: Phillips & Sampson, 1847.

64. Ellis, Joseph J. *His Excellency George Washington*. New York: Alfred A. Knopf, , 2004.

65. Leamon, James S. *Revolution Downeast: The War for American Independence in Maine*. Amherst: University of Massachusetts Press, 1993.

66. Gaustad, Edwin and Leigh Schmidt. *The Religious History of America*. San Francisco and New York: Harper, 2002.

67. Ulrich, Laurel Thatcher. *A Midwife's Tale: The Life of Martha Ballard, Based on Her Diary. 1785-1812*. New York: Vintage Books, 1990.

  Please see the 1997 PBS special based on this book -- a most beautiful production!

68. McCausland, Robert R. and Cynthia McCausland. *The Diary of Martha Ballard 1785-1812*. Camden, Maine: Picton Press, 1992.

69. McCullough, David. *1776*. New York: Simon and Schuster, 2005.

70. Hall, Rev. David B. Hall. *Halls of New England, Genealogical and Biographical*. Albany, New York: Joel Munsell's Sons, 1883.

71. National Archives, Washington, D.C. Papers of the Continental and Confederation Congress. *Nova Scotia Refugees Petition*. Feb. 25, 1784, (M247, Roll 53, Item 42, Vol. 2, pp. 412-414), Letter of Support signed by John Hancock and Samuel Adams; p. 416.

72. Thompson, Deborah. *Bangor, Maine 1769-1914: An Architectural History*. Orono, Maine: University of Maine Press, 1988.

73. Norton, Judith A. (compiled). *New England Planters in the Maritime Provinces of Canada*. Toronto: University of Toronto Press, 1985.

74. Taylor, Alan. *Liberty Men and Great Proprietors*. Chapell Hill & London: University of North Carolina Press, 1999.

References

75. Williamson, Joseph. *The Proposed Province of New Ireland.* Collections of the Maine Historical Society, Third Ser, I, 1901: pp. 147-157.

76. Thayer, Mildred N. *Brewer, Orrington, Holden Eddington: History and Families.* Brewer, Maine: Press of L. H. Thompson, Inc., 1962.

77. Buker, George E. *The Penobscot Expedition: Commodore Saltonstall and the Massachusetts Conspiracy of 1779.* Annapolis, Maryland: Naval Institute Press, 2002.

   Excellent documentation regarding the largest naval defeat in American history prior to Pearl Harbor, but I disagree with his conclusion. Dudley Saltonstall was the wrong commodore for this hastily planned expedition. He escaped with his life, but many of his men did not. Reading the British side to this tragedy, one has to conclude that Commodore "Sit-and-stall" (local parlance) was responsible for the loss of over forty vessels, loss of life, and great local suffering in the summer of 1779. Maine residents who chose to stay and fight suffered great horrors. The Massachusetts handling of this event laid the groundwork for Maine statehood in 1820.

78. Wood, John. "Seth Noble: Maugerville and the American Revolution." *Generation: The Journal of the New Brunswick Genealogical Society.* Summer 2007.

79. McGaw, Jacob. "Manuscript Sketch of Bangor." Maine Historical Society.

   Jacob McGaw (1778-1867) came to Bangor in 1805 to practice law. After his retirement from practice, he prepared this sketch regarding the early settlement of Bangor and deposited his work with the Maine Historical Society in Portland, Maine.

Index

Adams, John, 21, 83
Aiken, Daniel, 85
Allan, (Col.) John, 12, 15, 16, 17, 19, 20, 21, 22, 26, 84, 91
Alline, Henry, x
Allyn, Mrs. Joanna, 80
Arian, 29
Arminian, 29
Arminius, Jacobus, 29
Arnold, Benedict, 22
Ballard, Martha, 28, 64
Bangor City Council
   Incorporation ceremony (2003), 2
Bangor Daily News, 22, 59, 100
Bangor Incorporation Charter
   documents, 144-145, 116
   lost during War of 1812, 57
   signed into law, Feb. 25, 1791, 56
BANGOR TUNE, 115, 119, 121, 122, 123, 124, 125.
   (see Appendix 1), 97
Bangor, Maine
   revival of musical heritage along Penobscot River, 104
Bangor, Wales (UK), 1, 44, 66, 103, 186
Barker Family, ix, x, 9, 13, 52, 69
Barker, Jacob, 13
Barker, Joseph, viii
Barker, Noah, 48
Barrett, Rev. Elisha, 80
Bartholomew, Albert
   Seth and Hannah grandson, 87
Bartlett, Capt. Samuel, 38
Bauer, Susan A., 187
Beach, M.D., William Morrow, 88, 89

Beach, Uri, 88, 94
Bentley, Rev. William
   diary, 71, 72
Blackwood, James
   arrival in Dennysville, District of Maine, 54
Blaisdel, Richard Sanborn, 60
Boon Island,
   possible shipwreck site, 71
Boston Massacre, 10
Boyd, William, 38, 62, 74
Bradley, Levi, 39
Brewer, Col. John, 2, 31, 33, 36, 38
   headstone, 118, 170
   home, 38, 118, 169
   signature, 150, 151
British troops, 15, 19, 20, 21, 28, 90
British vessels, RAINBOW, BLONDE, MERMAID, HOPE, 18
Brooks, George, 38
Brooks, Robert C., 186
Buber, Polly, 11
Buck, Col. Jonathan, 38
Burpe, Salome, 11
Bussell, Isaac, 24
Bussell, Jacob, 24, 34, 39
Bussell, Jacob, Jr., 53
Calais, Maine, 2
Calvin, John, 29
Camden, District of Maine
   revolutionary war site, Clam Cove, 24
Chillicothe Supporter (Ohio), 94
Clark, David
   Seth and Hannah Noble descendant, 66
Colburn, Jeremiah, 36

Index

Colburn, William, 36, 106
Columbian Centinel (Boston), 71, 105
Columbus Dispatch, 95, 187
Columbus Metro Dispatch, 92
Cony, Dr. Daniel
    Boston trip for Seth Noble's Sunbury Petition (1787), 35
Coshocton and Mt. Vernon (Ohio), 87
Coy, Sarah, 10
Crosby, John, 38, 51
Crosby, Simon, 33, 39
Darby Township, Ohio, 89
Darling, Master and Commander Daniel
    SUSANNAH, 1795, 72
Deane, Rev. Samuele, 23
Dennett, Jacob, 39, 74
Dewey, Aaron, 11
Dublin, Ohio, 87
Dunk, George Montague
    Viscount of Sunbury, First Earl of Halifax, 4
Dyer, Capt. John, 17
Eddy, Col. Jonathan, 12, 13, 16, 25, 26, 32, 38, 48, 51, 52, 53, 84, 91, 108, 116, 149, 150, 151
Eddy, Dr. Robert
    Eddy family portrait, 150
Eddy, Elias, 26
Eddy, Frederick A.
    real story of "Col." Jona. Eddy portrait, 150
Eddy, Ibrook, 26
Eddy, William, 26
Emery, James, 60, 178
Esty, Israel, 11
Falmouth, 23, 97
Falmouth, 1775 burning of, 18
Farrington, John, 54
Fisher, Kenneth P., iii, 2, 117, 162, 185
Fort Cumberland, 12, 13, 20, 21

Fort Pine Hill, Camden, 24
Foster, Benjamin, 18
Fowler, Simeon, 33, 36, 38, 59
Frankfort, District of Maine, 39
Franklin County Historical Society, 93
Franklin County, Ohio, 85, 93, 117, 157
Franklinton (Columbus), Ohio, xi, 84, 85, 86, 87, 88, 89, 91, 92, 94, 117, 118, 156, 174, 175
Fredericton, NB, 4, 14
Gellison, Mr., 10
Gilman, Lt. Andrew, 24
Gorham, (British) Col. Joseph, 21
Gorham, Nathan, 88
Grant, (British) Gen. James, 21, 22
Granville, Ohio, 87
Greenleaf, Joseph, 20
Guthrie, Lolita
    Ohio Genealogical Society, 187
Halifax, Nova Scotia, 4, 11, 46
Hamlin, Sally and Polly, 28
Hampden County, Mass.
    birthplace of Seth Noble, 2, 11, 79, 177
Hancock, John, xv, 25, 26, 27, 28, 41, 42, 56, 116, 135, 146
Hancock. John, 43
Haselett, Rev. Mr., 28
Hasey, William, 62
Hayward, George, 187
Henry, Patrick, xiv, 8
Hichborn, Philip
    co-owner of the SUSANNAH, 73
Hichborn, Sr., Robert, 76
    death of and headstone, 77
    grieving father of Susan and Eliza, passengers aboard SUSANNAH, 76
    letter to cousin Paul Revere with great sorrow, 77
    owner of the SUSANNAH, 74

Holyoke, Capt. Jacob, 34
Holyoke, John, 38
Howard, Mary, 62
Howard, Thomas, 33, 39
Howland, Jeremiah, 11
Jefferson, President Thomas, 2, 84, 117, 158, 159
Johonnot, Col. Gabriel, 38
Jones, Hon. Stephen
    of Machias, 52
Karsten, Rev. Cannon Charles, 9
Kimball, Asa, 10
King George II, 2
King George III, 24, 37
King Sunneberie
    Saxon King (10th century), 4
Knapp, Rachel, 48, 50
Knapp, Sylvia
    passenger aboard the
        SUSANNAH, 111
Knox, Gen. Henry, 32
    wife Lucy (Flucker) Knox, 32
Lamper River, NH, 79
Lawrence, Gov. Charles, 4
Lee, John, 27, 36
Lincoln, Gen. Benjamin, 36, 54
Little, Rev. Daniel, 31, 33, 35, 36
Lord, Master and Commander John
    SUSANNAH, 1793, 72
Lovet, Capt., 10
Lowder, Col. Jonathan, 31, 36, 38, 39
Machias, 11, 13, 15, 16, 18, 19, 20, 38, 52, 55, 133, 134
Madison, Secretary of State James, 84, 117, 158, 159
Majabigwaduce, 27
Mann, Dr. Oliver, 27, 38
Martin, Joseph Plumb, 84
Mauger, Joshua, 3
Maugerville, vii, viii, ix, x, 3, 4, 5, 9, 13, 15, 18, 35, 43, 45, 47, 52, 65, 90, 94, 116, 117, 152, 166, 167, 178, 179, 181
Mead, Philip, 49, 115, 186
Miller, Abe and Frieda, 2

Mowat, (British) Lt. Henry, 18
Muskingum River (Ohio), 87
Musquash Cove, 15
Neptune, Francis Joseph, 18
Neptune, Orson, 37
Nevers, (Col. and Dr.) Phineas, 13, 26, 34
Nevers, Elisha, 13, 51
Nevers, Jonathan, 13, 26
New Hampshire Gazette, 70, 105
New Ireland, Province, District of
    Maine, 16, 198
New Worcester Plantation
    (today Orrington and Brewer), 33
Newark, Ohio, 87
Newbury Street (Bangor), 2, 13, 34, 47
Newburyport, Mass., 1, 3, 5, 11, 44, 98
Newfield, District of Maine, 79
Noble Ladies
    Florence Sihksnel, Joanne
        Schotthoefer, and Murphy, 2, 117, 160, 185
Noble, Ambassador John Joseph, vii, 13, 45, 52, 165, 184, 185, 186
Noble, Benjamin, vii, viii, ix, 34, 47, 52, 69, 93, 94
    almost died along trail to
        Canada, 52
    genealogy, 179, 181
Noble, Betsey, 61
    genealogy, 183
    married name Phillips, 94
Noble, Hannah, 52, 69
    daughter of Seth and Hannah
        (birth), 40
    death of Nathan Gorham, 88
    first husband Nathan Gorham, 88
    genealogy, 182
    interesting headstone in Amity,
        Ohio, 94
    married name Beach, 88

Index

photo, of Hannah (Noble) Beach, 163
Noble, Hannah (Barker), 9, 13, 26, 33, 34, 40, 43, 48
   death and burial, 47
   eulogy given by Seth, 48
   letter written to Seth during the war, 45
   song sung by Seth at her eulogy, 48
Noble, John Adams
   youngest son of Seth and Ruhama, 79, 88, 94, 184
Noble, Joseph, viii, ix, x, 26, 33, 47, 52, 69, 70, 93, 94, 180
   genealogy, 179
Noble, Medad, 11
Noble, Polly, 61, 69
   married name Atkins, 183
Noble, Sarah, 33, 47, 52, 66, 69
   genealogy, 180
   married name Bartholomew, 87, 94
Noble, Seth
   arrival in Kenduskeag Plantation, 33
   Bangor petition (1790), (see 140-143), 40, 41, 44, 116
   birth, 2
   church, Maugerville, 9, 117, 166
   church, newly discovered first site on Penobscot River, 53
   death of, 92, 93
   deposition (1777 Battle of Machias), 19
   diary entry, death of Seth, Jr, 71
   Eddington land grant (1785), 26
   escape from British, 13
   estate (Ohio), 94
   first ministry (Maugerville) NS, 3, 4
   first pastor, Montgomery, Mass., 79
   friends on Penobscot River, 38
   Hannah's death, 44, 48
   home and childhood, 3
   home, sites of in Bangor, 34
   installment on Kenduskeag Plantation. 1786, 32
   journey to Ohio, 85, 86, 87
   last sermon (Ohio), 91
   last sermon in Bangor (1797), 67
   letters written, 10, 23, 27, 51, 52, 53
   marriage Hannah Barker (see children, Seth, Jr., Joseph, Sarah, Benjamin, and Hannah Noble), 9
   marriage Mrs. Ruhama Emery (see children, Betsey, Polly, Thomas, and John Adams Noble), 59
   marriage to Mrs. Margaret (Mary) Riddle, 89
   military service, 17
   muster rolls, 115, 132, 133
   Noble St. (Columbus), 84, 175
   Ohio land grants, 84, 158, 159
   Old Franklinton Cemetery, 94, 95
   ordination (Newburyport), 3
   physical description, 80
   preached at Becket, Blandford, Feeding Hills, Ireland, Russell, and Springfield, MA, 79
   preached at Braintree and Hingham, Mass., 67
   preached eulogy for grieving families of SUSANNAH in Mass., 76
   preached eulogy for grieving families of the SUSANNAH at the Hichborn home in Stockton Springs, 76
   prominence of, 38

Index

residence in New Market, NH, 79
return to Bangor in 1799 for eulogy of the many sons and daughters who perished aboard the SUSANNAH, 113
revolutionary movement in Canada, 9, 12
Ruhama's death and burial, Pitcher Cem. Montgomery, Mass., 81
sermon (1774), 4, 5
Sophronia
 hymn tune by Isaac Watts, sung by Seth for Hannah, 48
Sunbury petition (1787), 34, 35, 116
Noble, Seth, Jr., 33, 52, 93, 107, 113, 179
death of, 71, 72, 79
Noble, Thomas
 infant son of Seth and Ruhama, 61
Northwest Territory, Ohio, 85
O'Brien, Jeremiah, 18
Ohio River, 86, 87
Oromoctou River, viii
Orono, Chief Joseph, 31, 36, 38
 death, 106
Page, James, 35
Palmer, 9
Passamaquoddy Natives, 18, 23, 38
Penn, William, 4
Penobscot Expedition, 1779, 23, 106, 154, 198
Penobscot Natives, 23, 35, 37
 Peol murder, 35
Perley, Major, 46
Pettingills, Esq., 29
Phelps, Edward, 88
Phelps, H. Warren, 88, 91
Portland, District of Maine, 18
Portland, Nova Scotia, 5
Potter, Alice, 10
Potter, Joseph, 74

Powers, Rev. Mr., 33
Predestination, 29
Putnam, Gen. Rufus, 86
Quebec, 11
Refugee Tract (Ohio)
 land grant for Nova Scotia patriots, 81, 90, 156
Renick, George and Felix, 86
Revere, Paul, xv, 44, 69, 72, 77, 78, 98, 109, 110, 112, 119
Rowe, Capt. Zebulon, 26
 Capt. Row, 11
Rowe, Zebulon Jr., 26
Rowley, Mass., 4, 9, 178
Salem Gazette, 71, 75, 105, 106
Salisbury, NH, 79
Sandusky, Ohio, 184
Sandy Bay
 Cape Ann, Mass. (shipwreck recovery site), 69, 70
Saunders, Thomas, 10, 11
Saveg/Savage, Capt., 28
Scioto River, 85, 86, 95, 174
Sewall, Henry, 29
Shepard, Rev. George, 48
Shute, Col. Benjamin, 38
Skinner, Dr. Elisha, 38
Smith, Florence Bishop
 an eternity of love and gratitude, 2, 50, 189
Sophronia
 hymn tune by Isaac Watts sung by Seth for Hannah, 48, 49, 115
St. Deinol
 Bangor, Wales (UK), site of earliest Christian monastery in British Isles, 103
St. John River, 3, 15, 17, 18, 52, 187
Stamp Act, 9
State Street (Bangor), 34, 47, 179, 189
Stillman, Major, 17
Stone, Jonathan

survey of Kenduskeag
Plantation (1786), 32
Stratham, NH, 79
Sullivant, Lucas
early Franklinton, Ohio settler,
85, 92, 96
Sunbury County, Nova Scotia
New Brunswick (after 1784), 3,
4
Sunbury Petition (1787)
(see p. 136), 116
Sunbury-on-Thames
county of Middlesex, England, 4
SUSAN AND ELIZA
vessel built after 1798 to honor
Hichborn daughters, 111
SUSANNAH
(see Chapter VI and Appendix
2), 70
built in Treat shipyard (below
Penjejawock Stream), 75
description of being built in
Bangor (1791), 74
first schooner built in Bangor
(1791), 72, 74
passenger list (see Appendix 2),
75
Tans'ur, William, 43, 97, 99, 102
The Oracle of the Day (Portsmouth,
NH), 71, 72, 105, 112
Thomas, Prof. Wyn

University of Wales, Bangor,
School of Music, 99, 102
Tibbets, Andrew, 10
Towns, Simeon, 10
Treat, Col. Robert, 33, 35, 38, 39,
51, 66, 74
Treat shipyard, 74, 105, 107
Treat, Robert, Jr., 75, 106
Ulmer, Capt. George, 24
Ulmer, Major Philip, 24
Waldo, Samuel, 32
Walhonding Indian trail (Ohio), 87
Washington, Gen. George, xiii, 12,
17, 21, 22, 23, 27, 54, 99, 188
Wasson, Mrs. and Daughter, viii,
14, 90
Watts, Dr. Isaac (1674-1748), 50,
100, 102, 115
Webster, Andrew, 33, 34, 38, 39,
41
daughter Prudence (wife of Wm.
Hasey), 61
wife Martha, 41
West, Capt. Jabez, 17
Westfield, Mass., viii, x, 2, 3, 11,
79, 81, 88, 115, 130
Whetstone (now Olentangy) River,
87
Whitney, Josiah, 11
Wilbraham, Mass., 5
Worthington, Ohio, 87, 88, 89, 184
Zanesville, Ohio, 87

www.ingramcontent.com/pod-product-compliance
Lightning Source LLC
Chambersburg PA
CBHW071229170426
43191CB00032B/1167